BEL MONDO

BEL MONDO

BEAUTIFUL WORLD
STEFANO MANFREDI
& JOHN NEWTON

Photography by James Pozarik
Design by Emery Vincent Design, Sydney

HODDER

A Hodder Book

Published in Australia and New Zealand in 2000
by Hodder Headline Australia Pty Limited
(A member of the Hodder Headline Group)
Level 22, 201 Kent Street, Sydney NSW 2000
Website: www.hha.com.au

National Library of Australia
Cataloguing-in-Publication data

Manfredi, Stefano, 1954.
bel mondo.

Includes index.
ISBN 0 7336 0996 1.

1. Cookery, Italian. 2. Cookery, Australian.

I. Newton, John (John Sefton).
II. Bel Mondo (Restaurant).
III. Title.

641.5945

Produced by Brewster Publishers Pty Ltd
Design by Emery Vincent Design, Sydney, Australia
Printed by Everbest, Hong Kong

For Isabella and Laura

CONTENTS

When painter Michelangelo Merisi from Caravaggio was under pressure once in 1604 he took it out on a Roman waiter, hurling a dish of artichokes at him and whacking the guy with the flat of his sword. It was April and the new season's artichokes were being eaten everywhere, as they are every April in Rome 400 years or so later. The man they called Caravaggio said the waiter was treating him like a two-bit crim, a particularly touchy matter for someone lately out of jail and scrabbling to retrieve his self-respect. He'd asked which of the artichokes were cooked in butter and which in oil, and the waiter had uncouthly stuck his nose into the dish to smell the difference.

A lot of the defining moments in life come at meal times: love and sudden death and all the critical difficulties in between. The food eaten at these special moments usually gets written out of the record, which is why knowing that Caravaggio lost it over the cooking of some artichokes is so precious. My theory on the artichokes is that he was looking for some home comfort in the butter-based cooking of the north, in an unhappy time, not wanting the more usual Roman oil cooking, and that this was why he was so susceptible to the waiter's grossness.

Caravaggio came from the north and what he brought to showy ideological Rome was a love of the painting of daily life and ordinary people, a grounding in the unpretentious naturalism of the Bergamo and Brescia parts of Lombardy, a solidly realistic style that pervades all of his work. It seemed revolutionary in the mannered and artificial world of Rome.

Stefano Manfredi comes from Brescia too, and to flash eclectic Sydney he and his mother Franca have brought the same values of Lombard realism to their cooking. Nothing mannered, nothing there for show, no forced marriages of weird ingredients. And Franca's exquisite gnocchi are done with sage and burnt butter, not oil. But the quiet northern realities behind Caravaggio's art were transformed into something stronger and stranger when the painter met the cosmopolitan opulence of Rome, something more voluptuous and more dangerous and more demanding, and Manfredi cuisine is far more than transplanted down-home values. It has seized the new possibilities that Australian and Pacific produce offer. It has created an art of cooking that is genuinely new and so much itself that calling it Italian or Australian or anything in between seems to miss its point. There are no abalone in Brescia.

And you never find *bel mondo* waiters sniffing the food as they bring it to the table, though you may encounter the odd unruly customer. This quite gripping text is no mere recipe book. It reaches beyond the food to the whole theatre of work and play that every restaurant becomes. It reminds you of the social drama of our nourishment. *bel mondo* at full rhythm is total theatre, and the diners are a part of the unfolding drama.

The other day I called Stefano on his cell phone in the middle of the afternoon, and I couldn't hear his voice for all the bangs and shrieks. Even at *bel mondo* they lose the plot occasionally, I thought with a kind of relief. But Steve was on the dodgems with his daughter, on the other side of the harbour. Cooks need their day of rest, and Steve was getting away from it all at Luna Park. ■

PETER ROBB

Peter Robb's most recent book is *M*, about the life, death and art of the painter Michelangelo Merisi from Caravaggio. He is also the author of *Midnight in Sicily*, a book of art, food, crime and history that *The Economist* called 'quite simply, the best book in English about Italy'.

INTRODUCTION

Restaurants are fragile, artificial fantasies from a restaurateur's most beautiful dream. They are places of comfort, solace and theatre where one can experience life at its most bizarre and at its most sublime.

The restaurateur's craft is one of the most noble and yet at times most demeaning and if you had not already guessed, the restaurant is one of life's many contradictions. It is a place where people create life-long attachments and life-long enemies. It is a place where deals are made and pacts are founded, where events are marked and indeed where life is celebrated. All this and more within the most basic of rituals – eating.

All the while you are looked after. Your pleasure and comfort is the business of all who work there, from the person who has taken your call to the one who has taken out the empty bottles to place them neatly in the darkness after all have left. At the heart of this book is both the physical space of *bel mondo* and the characters, the team that makes it run. My heartfelt thanks to all whom have given part of their lives to make this creature breathe.

My thanks and respect to my partners – Franca, Julie and Franck who have fed this restaurant with total commitment and passion.

As John, my co-author, has pointed out this is the third book on which we have collaborated. His insights and fascination with restaurants, especially the people who inhabit them, have brought a lot to this book. He has taught me always to ask why and to not be satisfied with the most obvious.

With this book, we wanted to give you, the reader, an insight into the life of *bel mondo* – a bit like a voyeur's window. Not only have we included the polish we work so hard to achieve but also the gangly, seedy, not-so-perfect bits that hang out of every restaurant. It's certainly not a how to do it, step by step sort of guide. If there were a formula for a successful restaurant, it would have been discovered long ago. In part we wanted to add to the pool of knowledge on the subject. ∎

STEFANO MANFREDI

INTRODUCTION

This is the third book I've done with Stefano Manfredi (the second, also with his mother Franca, has yet to be released), and all three experiences have been almost too much like good fun to be work.

What happens is Steve and I sit down, his place or mine, and we talk. We talk and talk. Transcripts of the Manfredi-Newton tapes will be interesting reading in the distant future. Steve's complete dedication to his craft – cooking – is only matched by his immersion in restaurant lore, legend and gossip. These transcripts will be locked away for at least 15 years. Dangerous stuff.

This has been by far the most interesting book to work on. *Fresh From Italy* gave me the insight I needed into the migrant experience to be able to go away and write *Wogfood*. Talking about cooking with Franca was better

than 12 months studying in Italy. But this book has been fascinating for many reasons. Its dissection of the restaurant industry as a whole; the way it provides an insight into how a truly great restaurant like *bel mondo* actually works and continues to pump out, with deceptive ease, wonderful and unforced food seven days and nights a week.

And, finally, the way we worked through context: putting *bel mondo* in its place in the restaurant renaissance that has happened in the New World (and in culinary terms, England is part of that New World) in the last quarter of the second millennium.

This book has also been somewhat easier because, while I said when we did *Fresh From Italy* that Steve and I complemented each other perfectly – he was a better cook than he was a writer and I was vice versa – in the ensuing seven years he has become not just a competent writer, but a good one. And a lot of that is

evidenced in the text. I'm afraid I can't report a similar advance in my cooking skills.

I want to thank the owners and staff at *bel mondo* for putting up with a snoopy writer hanging around the kitchen and the office asking a bunch of stupid and intrusive questions and generally getting in the way. Most especially I want to thank Julie Manfredi-Hughes and Franca Manfredi, both of whom I'm privileged to call friends; Franck Crouvezier, Franco Manfredi, Sally Hunter, Gabby Hunt, Cathy Montebello, and a special thanks to Linda Maynard, the best transcriber we've found in seven years. And, of course, Steve, who has taught me more than he will ever know. ∎

JOHN NEWTON

"EVERYONE HAS TO KNOW THEIR ROLE AND THEIR SCRIPT. IF YOU FORGET YOUR LINES, OR GET IT WRONG, YOU STEAL THE MAGIC FROM THE DINER." JULIE MANFREDI HUGHES

1

MOVEMENT

"YOU HAVE MADE A DECISION TO EAT AT A RESTAURANT..."

You have made a decision to eat at a restaurant in four days time. It is a Sunday, and you are planning this event for the following Thursday night. Let us say you live in Sydney, Australia, which is, according to those who profess to know, at the time of writing, one of the finest places in the world in which to make such a decision. American power chef Jeremiah Tower said after a visit in 1997 that, as far as he was concerned, when it came to restaurant dining, Paris and New York were 'mere suburbs of Sydney'.

At the very least, there is an increasingly sophisticated and growing audience for fine food in Sydney. And a proliferation of restaurants to feed that audience's hunger – around 3000 not including cafes or hotel dining rooms. But in whatever large, modern city you live (Sydney has a population of some 4 million) the proportions will be much the same, even if the obsession with dining out is not evident.

Your decision is not, therefore, a simple one. You must first narrow down your decision to a restaurant that will be open on a Thursday night (still trading and, hopefully, not for sale), and have an available table with enough chairs for your party. But that's just logistics. Next, the hard questions.

What are your criteria? Why will you choose one restaurant over another? What is it that moves you towards a rendezvous with pleasure at restaurant A rather than restaurants B, C, D, E or F? Because that movement has been set in place by the decision to dine out. From that moment, if all goes according to plan, you will travel from your home to the restaurant and there will be a table set with crisp linen, sparkling cutlery and eagerly empty wine glasses, waiting just for you. You will be expected. You may even, if you are known to the chef or restaurateur, be anticipated: there could well be a file on you, noting that you have a fondness, say, for a margarita before dinner, or that you always order offal.

Because this is no cheap night out. This is no 'let's go down the road for a quick snack because I can't be bothered cooking.' This is 'Let us go to a place where we will feel comfortable and cosseted. Where the environment

and the service as much as the food will conspire to transport us from the renovations that have turned our home into a building site/the job that is making my life into a nightmare/ the children who are, at this moment, driving us mad and if the babysitter wants them she can have them.' An environment that will stimulate conversation, reminiscence, even enjoyable social argument.

You plan to dine with friends. Dining out with friends is far more comfortable than dining in with friends. There is no stress. The cook is almost certainly better than you. You can give yourself entirely to the company without worrying about whether the duck breasts under the griller will be properly pink; whether the next bottle you open (the last of the '94 Salitage Pinot Noir) will be corked and you will have to fall back on that cheap stuff you keep at the back of the cupboard. Because at the restaurant if the wine is corked they will bring you another bottle and another until they find one that is not corked. Ditto with the duck.

It goes without saying that you are not planning to make a rendezvous to meet at a restaurant with friends in four days time because you are hungry. No. Increasingly, restaurants are our public spaces. We go to them to seduce and propose, to seal deals and to carouse, for gatherings and celebrations of family and social importance. Eating, once their prime reason for being, is now only one part of the equation. The restaurant (and the cafe) is more than a place, it's a tool: to borrow a phrase from Jesuit philosopher Ivan Illich, a tool for conviviality.

To choose just one, you may decide to consult the form, something like the *Good Food Guide* (most big cities have one similar), and count hats and scores. You may discuss the issue with friends at work, your wife, husband or lover. You may consult a friend who is an acknowledged expert in making these choices.

Your decision may be very simple. You may opt to go to the place that you always go to, a place where you feel comfortable enough to walk in, remove your coat, sit down and place only one order, 'bring food and drink',

"PARADOXICALLY, I AM MOST *AT-HOME* IN A RESTAURANT. NO, THIS IS WRONG – MORE PRECISELY, I LIKE BEING IN A RESTAURANT BECAUSE IT IS WHERE I FEEL NOT-IN-ANY-WAY-SHAPE-OR-FORM AT-HOME."

FRANK MOORHOUSE

》

having total faith in the kitchen, the cellar and the restaurateur's ability to choose that which pleases you. If so, you are very lucky. The Greeks have a word for such a place, they call it a 'steki'.

You may, as some cautious and meticulous diners do, solicit quotes. Call several restaurants and ask them to fax or email their menus, with prices. You may ring and quiz the restaurant on its menu for the night you have chosen. The fanatically fastidious may wish to do as the English restaurant critic Lieutenant Colonel Nathaniel Newnham-Davis did, and visit a chosen restaurant to interview the manager or the maître d', preferably the former. The good Lieutenant Colonel asserted that 'the more intelligent help you will get ... the more certain you are to have an artistic meal, and not be spending your money unworthily.'

Or you may narrow the choice because of some food preference: you feel like northern Chinese, Moghul Indian, Italian, traditional Thai. Or one of your party may be subject to one of the increasingly prevalent food phobias: no red meat, no offal, no gluten, no frogs legs, in which case practicality will narrow down the field.

Hopefully, all four of you have the sense to be omnivores and are wide open to food type. As long as it is excellent. Now is the time to switch hats, and view this dilemma from the restaurateur's point of view. Because as any restaurateur knows, at any time of the day or night diners are choosing in exactly the way described above, and success or failure depends solely on enough of them choosing a chair in their restaurant.

But let us show you how we, the owners of *bel mondo*, have been able to persuade enough people to choose our chairs, tables and plates in two locations, under

three names, since 1983, for us to continue in the restaurant business and to prosper modestly.

We were, when we first opened in 1983, entirely innocent of one simple truth: a restaurant is a brand. A successful brand is one that has a clearly defined personality, and fulfils a need. Such a brand will always persuade people to move towards it.

We were, then, under the impression that if we cooked well, people would flock to eat our food. The initial success of what was called, back in those days, The Restaurant (later the Restaurant Manfredi), was due to a stroke of luck, something beyond the control of any involved. The two original chefs still in the kitchen, Franca Manfredi and her son Stefano, were born in Italy in Lombardy, the little town of Gottolengo. Our aim was to transpose the cooking

of Franca and her mother, Angelina, to the restaurant dining table.

We weren't restaurateurs back then, we were cooks (the great journey since then has been learning how to run a restaurant properly) and as such we were thoroughly kitchen focused. This meant that we had a culinary heritage genetically installed, and there was no need to ask the question most New World chefs have to ask themselves when they walk into a kitchen: what am I going to cook?

That geographical stroke of luck was twofold in that Italian food, along with Chinese, is the world's most popular cuisine. From the very beginning, we had a strong identity, not just national – Italian, but regional – Lombard. So that when prospective diners begin to think about where to dine, when the name *bel mondo* enters into play they have a very clear idea of what that means. ∎

BEL MONDO MOMENTS

THE DRUNKS

...Friday lunch traditionally is the longest lunch of the week. A customer who had been coming regularly for lunch was entertaining two colleagues. They'd had a good time, spending around $1000, and had enjoyed a few bottles of very good wine. It was now 7.00 pm. They were still there and beginning to get a little loud and were obviously losing control. The first of the early dinner tables were in and were a little put off by the behaviour of these three unwise diners. Diplomatically, our sommelier asked the gentlemen if they would like to move to the bar, as we needed to set their table for a dinner booking. Ignoring this request, the host asked for another bottle of wine. The sommelier calmly stated that *bel mondo* has a duty of care to its customers and that it would be negligent of him to supply any more alcohol. In a matter of minutes the three were shown to a taxi and were taken home. The following Monday our sommelier received a call from the host's personal assistant complaining about their treatment and asking why were they refused service when they had spent so much money. The secretary was taken through the story and assured that money was not the main concern. She was more than understanding and hinted that this was not out of character. Her employer has yet to return to *bel mondo*.

Oscar Wilde once said: 'In matters of grave importance, style, not sincerity, is the vital thing.'

Style has nothing to do with fashion (fashion is the momentary, surface gloss on style), but is the accumulated essence of your being. It has to do with understanding who you are.

Because of our birthright we know who we are, how we shall cook and serve food and how we shall treat our clients. That clarity has been with us from the very early days, when we opened in a dingy back lane in a then unfashionable corner of the city. It was that clarity, combined with a fair sized serving of luck, that contributed to our early success.

But what does a restaurateur without the genetic advantage of being born Italian or Chinese or Thai or French do? Find a base.

Think about the successful restaurateurs in your city. When you look at the person, the restaurant and the life, there is a seamlessness between them that is the essence of style.

In Sydney, the name that springs to mind is David Thompson. His classic Thai cuisine is fed by his constantly revisiting the site of his original inspiration so that he can absorb what is happening to it there in a far more thorough way than the Thai-born chef who repeats the techniques handed down to him by his heritage. In David's case, his clarity of culinary vision is a result of his having chosen to cook Thai from the very depths of his – Australian – being.

When prospective diners begin to think about where to dine, names will run through their head. There will be a list, and you must be on that list. That takes clarity of vision, time, persistence, luck and a knowledge of your customer.

Knowing your customers means a lot more than an evening post service promenade around the tables by a chef having changed thoughtfully into a clean white jacket. When first we opened in the back lane, we did so for two reasons. The rent was cheap, and we were quite close to a large newspaper office. For us, having Fairfax nearby kept us alive

throughout the lean times. It was fortunate for us that journalists liked lunch. Friday lunch eventually turned into a long and often arduous task for various of the senior journalists from this organisation, many of whom had a problem with endings: lunch could and often did re-emerge as dinner. We are fairly certain that a record set in 1988 at The Restaurant, for the longest lunch by a Fairfax journalist, still stands, as does the journalist concerned. From our point of view, other diners needed to be warned, in advance, of the often raucous behaviour of these very important customers, and staff needed to be able to keep a firm but friendly hand on them.

This kind of customer knowledge is invaluable. The restaurant will become a part of the lives of these people and they will follow you when and if you have to move. ∎

"THE BEGINNING AND THE ROOT OF ALL GOOD IS THE PLEASURE OF THE STOMACH; EVEN WISDOM AND CULTURE MUST BE REFERRED TO THIS."
EPICURUS

PAESE CHE VAI, RICETTE CHE TROVI. IN EACH TOWN ONE TRAVELS, THERE IS ALWAYS A NEW RECIPE FOR THE SAME DISH.

(FROM THE ITALIAN KITCHEN)

Restaurants are like clubs; they are more than a place where one goes to eat. Hunger is only a small part of the equation. More and more they become places where specific languages are spoken and particular rituals are performed. The more ease with which a restaurant can instruct their clientele on their particular culture, the more enthusiastic and willing the diner is to belong to the club.

For example, regulars at *bel mondo* know that instead of butter, they are given rich green olive oil to accompany their bread. No side plate is provided so that the damask cloth is littered with crumbs. The rituals are different in other restaurants.

But what is it that makes us behave like regulars, going back time after time to a restaurant? The answer is simple, but the way a restaurant achieves it is the hard part. It is a performance. The waiters and the kitchen staff are some of the actors. Even the clientele to varying degrees are part of the show, however, unlike the kitchen and floor staff of the restaurant, their parts are mostly unscripted.

The script has to be interesting and above all have a mysterious quality to it that sets it apart from other performances around town. The parts played by the clients must make them look and feel good and, because it is mostly unscripted, must be very easy to follow.

The food is no small part of the show but, as has been proven time and again, it is not enough to have a great cook in the kitchen. There has to be woven into the fabric of every great restaurant, no matter how humble or how grand, a mixture of food, performance and mystery.

This last ingredient is the least intangible: let's call it the plot. In this context, 'plot' can be defined as the sum total of the delivery of all the other ingredients to the diner in a meaningful way. Such a plot can only be woven by a skilful restaurateur. How many times have we seen great food in a beautiful environment fail because of the lack of a cohesive plot? Because the parts played by all the characters, diners and employees remain a mystery to all concerned?

"The interior of a restaurant, examined in some detail, offers to the keen eye of the philosopher a spectacle well worth his interest, on account of the variety of situations contained within it." JEAN ANTHELME BRILLAT-SAVARIN

The final intangible element of mysterious alchemy can only be achieved if the food has risen to the appropriate level for the restaurant's clientele and if the performance of the staff is polished to the point where everyone knows their role and has rehearsed their lines. The performance includes both kitchen and dining room. The connection between food and service must appear seamless and effortless.

To this end it is not the chef but the dining room conductor who is responsible. It is the ease with which clients are greeted, relaxed and made to feel part of the performance that determines whether they are then going to enjoy the food. It is rare that people will like the food if they have had lousy service.

The 1980s were mostly about the rise of chefs as stars. As a consequence many restaurants had brilliant food but the service was incredibly substandard. The 1990s have already seen a polishing of the performance, and restaurateurs have gravitated toward what theatre directors call 'focus', all the parts of the performance becoming synchronised and harmonious.

To a great extent Gay Bilson was one of the first of the 'modern Australians' to realise the importance of performance enhanced food. Berowra Waters Inn was often described as the quintessential Australian dining experience, where all the elements came together harmoniously. She in turn influenced a whole new generation of 'performance directors' that are now in restaurants all over.

It is easy to say what causes a restaurant to fail, and there are countless critics doing this every day all over the world. What makes a restaurant succeed will always remain a mystery because, like a work of art or a play, it depends upon so many diverse elements all coming together to mean something to the individual. It is this connection with the patron that determines the success of a restaurant as a dining experience and the willingness of that patron to feel part of the 'club'.

To sum up: know who you are; know what you are going to cook; know your customers; and let the show begin.

We are now at the point where you are, once again, the customer who wants a table for four on a Thursday night. But you have progressed: you are now ready to choose *bel mondo*. Your first move is towards the telephone, to a telephone call that sets in motion a chain of events. Practical considerations. The four chairs must be free. A system must be in place so that, four days from the call, when you and your friends walk in the maître d' on duty knows who you are. That telephone call is the beginning of the dining experience.

All employees should be trained thoroughly in the art of taking a booking. For example, when first we moved to our present location, we were overwhelmed with custom. For a time, it was extremely difficult to get a table in *bel mondo*. As much as this was flattering, it presented problems. Julie put it this way: 'I instilled in the reservation staff that we must be grateful for that and every other call, be grateful that we're in demand. We were on a bit of a high there, we were hot stuff, and I wanted to discourage the hubris that can accompany that. I figure the moment you get carried away with that, you're dead in the water.'

And now the night has come. You, your companion, and your two friends have met and have moved from your homes to our restaurant. You have been anticipating this moment for days. That is a danger. Anticipation can lead to inflated – and easily deflated – expectations. This is a defining moment. You arrive at the front door. You enter. What happens in the next five minutes will decide whether you have a good time or a bad time, a good meal or a bad meal. Before you've been seated, before you've been handed the menus, that is so often when the decision is made. ■

Walk in the front door. Stop. Stand still for a moment, and forget yourself. Put all that me-me-me stuff out of your head (How do I look? Does anybody here know me? Am I dressed right?) and let your antennae quiver. A restaurant should fit you like a well cut jacket. It should be comfortable, and feel good to be in. There's no point in going to the latest hot joint if it's going to make you feel m i s e r a b l e

JOHN NEWTON

Now you are standing at the door, having just pushed through it. This first contact between yourself and the waiter or maître d' is of utmost importance.

It doesn't seem to matter how sophisticated, how experienced a diner is, he or she can be crushed, offended, devastated by the deliberate or inadvertent rudeness of a waiter. What is today called 'attitude'.

At *bel mondo* there is a waiter assigned to the front door during service. As soon as you enter, you are greeted, led to the waiter's station, and handed over to the maître d'. There, you will proffer your name and your table will be confirmed. Your coats will be taken by the waiter who greeted you. You will be asked if you want to go to the bar for a drink, or straight to your table. Whatever you decide to do, your account is opened, and you are now in our hands.

This whole process is conducted smoothly, a ballet. Moving through the front door of a restaurant, you have left the outer world, left behind the prosaic, the everyday, and moved into another world, a theatre in which you are at once audience and participant. Any good restaurant offers this fantastic (in the original sense of the word) transition. You must feel you have arrived, and that where you have arrived is the centre of the world.

WAITERNOIA

In her curiously churlish and joyless book *Dining Out,* Joanne Finkelstein quotes several written instances of the difficult relations between diner and waiter. Typical is an article from *The Age* in 1984 by English journalist Clement Freud. 'Today's waiter has taken it upon himself to be the front man for the chef, the arbiter of taste and etiquette in the dining room, with a demonic brief to ensure that the customer never feels sufficiently at ease to behave badly.' You could argue that things have changed a lot since 1984, but we would argue that even at their worst, waiters have never be-haved to the level of Mr Freud's paranoic delusions. And no, the tone of the article is not humorous; he is deadly serious.

Ms Finkelstein, in her conclusion, states that 'the exercise of power between the personnel of the restaurant and the diner ensures there is an imbalance which disadvantages the diner'. You begin to suspect that her book is the result of a bad experience she had with a waiter as a child. She should have been reminded of Nancy Cunard's assertion that 'no one can make you feel inferior without your permission'.

In a chapter entitled 'The Waiting Game' in his book *The Man Who Ate Everything*, Jeffrey Steingarten writes of having enrolled in something called the New York Professional Service School. Now, this entire chapter may be fictional tongue in cheek, but if so, it would be out of character with the rest of the book. He was there, he writes, to 'be initiated into the secret stratagems that waiters use to infuriate us, ruin our dinner and take us to the cleaners'. And, in the hands of someone he calls Philippe, that is exactly what he learns. Philippe outlines to Steingarten and the other aspiring waiters his opinion of the diners who come into a restaurant: 'You can do whatever you want with them – they are Play-Doh in your hands.'

Two of the partners at *bel mondo* are, or were, waiters. We are mystified by the persistence and entrenched nature of this condition that we have decided to call 'waiternoia'. Where does it come from? Is it a manifestation of deeply seated feelings of inadequacy? Social unease at all levels? Is it regression to a childhood fear of the person who carried the food: Mummy is in charge and we are out of control? Who knows. We offer it to any analyst reading this book as the subject for a fascinating paper. We know some very nice waiters. We have also known some horrors. We do not employ them. We have never employed, nor would we, someone like 'Philippe'. Maybe that's the difference between New York and Sydney. ∎

...PLAY-DOH IN YOUR HANDS...

THE CODFATHER

The experts told fish farmer Bruce Malcolm he couldn't do it, that the Murray cod is territorial, highly aggressive and so not suitable for aquaculture. It's a good thing he took no notice.

The movement of this fish onto our menu began in 1990, in Grong Grong in the Riverina district in southern New South Wales. Bruce had been hatching freshwater fish for release as fingerlings into farm dams for recreational angling and selling silver perch to commercial farmers to raise the money to continue his life's work, solving the problems of farming the Murray cod.

When he talks about these fish, a reverence creeps into his voice: 'It's not only Australia's largest freshwater fish, but a truly majestic and magnificent animal.' And the stuff of legends.

It's a particularly unattractive fish with a large mouth armed with formidable rows of teeth, and it can grow up to 113 kg in weight and 1.83 m in length (the largest on record). All around south-eastern Australia, tall tales are told in pubs and angling clubs of titanic struggles with old man cod - how, for instance, one was caught using a whole kangaroo on a meat hook as bait.

But what interests us here is the flavour of a fish that was a major food source to pre-colonial Aborigines and was highly prized by the first European settlers. Marine biologist Nick Ruello reckons the Murray cod is the marine equivalent of Kobe beef: 'they lay down big lumps of fat in their bellies and have the fish equivalent of marbling.' In the wild, their diet consists of freshwater crays, yabbies, shrimp, frogs, water fowl, small mammals, tortoises and other reptiles. To find the right diet for the farmed fish, Bruce said 'we looked at what they ate in the wild – and at what kind of animal they are, a high order carnivore'.

Because it's not a highly active fish - it tends to eat voraciously then sit around quietly digesting – Bruce says that 'it retains most of its natural flavour.'

For some time, the Murray cod had been hovering on the edge of critically low stocks due to a whole variety of causes to do with the side effects of the regulation of the Murray-Darling river system and, from about 1970 on, the invasion of the river system by huge numbers of carp. At first the Murray cod enjoyed a feed of carp, but eventually, the 'rabbit of the river' outbred them.

Bruce Malcolm introduced his farmed cod at a gathering of chefs and food writers in Mudgee in May 1998 after eight years work. The chefs included Luke Mangan of Salt in Sydney, Ralph Potter of Darleys in the Blue Mountains and Michael Manners of Selkirk's in Orange. All were enormously impressed.

Michael Manners said it was the best fish to come on the market since Atlantic salmon.

bel mondo took delivery of four of the first two-year-old fish and immediately put them on the menu, roasting the fish and serving it with boiled kipfler potatoes with parsley, accompanied by a rich stock of the bones with a little tomato and chilli. It was immediately popular, and now appears regularly. ■

...THE STUFF OF LEGENDS...

Suddenly you are seated. Within minutes, you should have bread, olive oil and olives, and then the menu. If you have moved from your home to this place, then many of the items on the menu have moved in time and place great distances to be there on that menu.

Dishes like Franca Manfredi's celebrated gnocchi (having come down in time as a recipe from Franca's mother, Angelina, herself a celebrated cook), like the tortelli di zucca (the pumpkin tortelli, a dish from the north, especially Mantova, Lombardy, the Veneto and Piemonte) have then, as did so many dishes,

migrated with their custodians to a new land and survived, relatively intact. Sometimes, unexpected problems arise in transition. As with the pumpkin for the tortelli. Let Franca explain.

'The pumpkins are not as good as they are in Italy. There, in autumn, we'd buy a special pumpkin, Americanine, and leave it on top of the roof outside, and it would season through the snow and the rain. If it was too fresh, it was not very good, it had to stay outside for a couple of months to dry out.

'If you do that here, after a couple of weeks, it often goes rotten. But sometimes I buy a pumpkin and it's a good pumpkin and I tell Stefano and he rings

up and says give me one bag of good pumpkins, and I leave them out, but I have to check them all the time to make sure they're not going rotten. Here I use the Queensland blue. I found they're quite good.

'The problem with the pumpkin here is they have too much water. You have to try to get rid of the water. To make tortelli, you have to steam it, you can't bake it because you get the skin going dry.

'I tried everything possible to get rid of the water. I even went to the showground during the show they have once a year where the machinery is sold, and they said there's nothing to separate the water from the pumpkin.'

"Cooks draw goodness from forests, gardens, seas and markets ... and then bring us together at hearth, village, square and restaurant to share."
MICHAEL SYMONS

Franca has solved the problem of the pumpkin – but how, is her secret.

But even some of the dishes using Australian ingredients have travelled over great distances to arrive on the menu. In 1999 for example, we began serving Murray cod, a legendary freshwater fish from southern Australia that had, before being successfully farmed, been all but wiped out of its natural habitat.

MOVEMENT BEGINS THIS BOOK, BECAUSE IT IS THE MOVEMENT OF FOOD, OF DINERS, OF WAITERS, EVEN OF FASHION, THAT BRINGS US TOGETHER. AND NOW YOU HAVE MOVED INTO OUR WORLD, YOU ARE SEATED, WITH A MENU IN HAND. THE SHOW IS ABOUT TO BEGIN.

RECIPES

BISCOTTINI DI PARMIGIANO

Makes 30-40

We serve these tasty little biscotti with different kinds of olives as people arrive. They are perfect for whetting the appetite.

125g salted butter
250g plain flour
80g grated parmesan cheese
1 whole egg
pinch salt

In a food processor, blend all the ingredients together until they are well incorporated. Do not overwork. Form the dough into a sausage shape about the diameter of a 20 cent piece and rest in the refrigerator for 1 hour. Preheat the oven to 180°C. Cut the dough into disks 2-3 mm thick and place on a baking sheet. Cook for 10-12 minutes until a light golden colour. Allow to cool then serve, or store in an airtight container.

BRAISED CANNELLINI BEANS

Serves 6-8 as a first course

5 tablespoons extra virgin olive oil
2 carrots, peeled and chopped into half rounds
1 stick celery, sliced into 5 mm sections
1 medium onion, chopped
3 medium-sized ripe tomatoes, peeled and
chopped
1 cup dry white wine
500g cannellini beans, soaked overnight
3 cloves garlic, minced
large handful parsley, finely chopped
sprig each basil and thyme
salt and pepper

Place the olive oil in a saucepan with the carrots, celery and onion and fry gently until the vegetables have softened. Add the tomatoes and the wine, bring to the boil and then add the beans. Simmer for 10 minutes then add the garlic, parsley, basil and thyme. Simmer until the beans are cooked, season to taste and serve with bread and polenta.

POLENTA AND PARMESAN TORTA WITH A PICCATA OF CHICKEN LIVERS AND ONIONS

Serves 6 as a first course

1.25 litres salted water
250g polenta
150g parmesan, grated
3 medium onions, thinly sliced
extra virgin olive oil
$1/4$ cup dry white wine
salt and pepper
$1/4$ cup young flat-leaf parsley
6 rashers prosciutto, thinly sliced
12 fat chicken livers, cleaned

Bring the salted water to the boil. Add the polenta in a fine stream, stirring constantly so that no lumps form. Keep stirring until the polenta starts to come away from the sides of the saucepan. Turn down the heat to a very low simmer, cover the saucepan with a lid and cook for about 25 minutes, stirring well every 5 minutes or so. When it is ready, whisk in the parmesan, turn the mixture out into a rectangular tray and allow it to set – it should be about 2 cm thick. Once cool, cut it into squares about 5-6 cm wide. These will keep in the refrigerator until needed.

Place the onions in a small saucepan with 2 tablespoons of olive oil and the white wine. Simmer for about 30 minutes or until soft and jammy. Season to taste and add the parsley. Heat 5 tablespoons of olive oil in a pan and fry the prosciutto for about 10 seconds on each side until crisp. In the same oil, gently fry the chicken livers.

To serve the dish, reheat the polenta square in a microwave or a preheated 180°C oven for a few minutes then place it in the centre of the plate. Spoon some onion on, then the chicken livers and finally the prosciutto. Serve immediately.

HARBOUR PRAWNS WITH OX-HEART TOMATO AND PESTO

Serves 6 as a first course

young rocket leaves
72 cooked harbour prawns, peeled, tails left on
extra virgin olive oil
salt and pepper
3 medium ox-heart tomatoes, washed, topped
and tailed, halved
150 ml pesto (see recipe this page)

Dress the rocket leaves and prawns with the olive oil and season with salt and pepper. Place the ox-heart tomatoes on each plate. Add a little pesto on top, then some rocket leaves and 12 prawns per person. Drizzle some pesto around the base of the tomato and serve.

PESTO

Makes about 250g

3 cloves garlic
85g pine nuts, lightly roasted
3 large handfuls basil leaves
100 ml extra virgin olive oil
8 tablespoons grated parmesan
salt

Place the garlic, pine nuts and basil in a food processor. Pulse until the ingredients start to break up. Add the olive oil gradually until it is all incorporated. Mix in the parmesan, season to taste and store in the refrigerator until it is to be used.

GENOVESE-STYLE FISH AND SHELLFISH STEW

Serves 6 as a first course

2 litres fish and shellfish stock (see recipe this page)
1 cup fresh tomato sauce (see recipe this page)
12 mussels, cleaned
2 small octopus, cut into single legs
6 prawns, shelled and deveined
3 crabs, cleaned and quartered
6 scallops
1 medium-sized calamari, cleaned and cut into bite-sized pieces
300g assorted fish (cod, salmon, whiting, perch) cut into bite-sized pieces
salt and pepper
6 tablespoons pesto (see recipe page 33)

Bring the stock and the tomato sauce to the boil in a saucepan. Poach all the seafood together in the broth, making sure that it is not overcooked. Season to taste and distribute among the plates. Drizzle with a tablespoon of pesto in each plate to finish, then serve.

FISH AND SHELLFISH STOCK

Makes 5 litres

prawn shells, some fish heads and bones
2 celery sticks, roughly chopped
1 carrot, roughly chopped
2 leeks, cleaned and cut into thick chunks
6 ripe tomatoes, peeled and chopped
parsley, roughly chopped
salt and pepper to taste

Place the prawn shells, fish heads and bones, vegetables, tomatoes and parsley in a large stockpot that will fit everything comfortably. Cover with plenty of cold fresh water and bring to a simmer. Keep simmering for 1-1 1/2 hours, then strain. Reduce if it is not intense enough, then season to taste.

FRESH TOMATO SAUCE

Makes 1.5 litres

2 kg ripe tomatoes
1/4 cup extra virgin olive oil
2 leeks, washed and sliced into rings
4 cloves garlic, minced
handful basil leaves
salt and pepper

Peel the tomatoes by immersing them in boiling water for about 30 seconds. The skin should come away very easily with the help of a small paring knife. Chop them roughly and keep them aside in a bowl. Heat the oil in a pot, then add the leeks and garlic. Simmer gently for about 5 minutes until the leeks are soft. Add the chopped tomatoes and cook for as long as you like. If you want a fresh flavour then just cook for 10-15 minutes, but if you want the flavour to be more intense, cook the sauce longer. Add the basil leaves at the end. Season and it is ready to use.

ROAST MURRAY COD WITH SPINACH, SULTANAS AND PINE NUTS

Serves 6 as a main course

olive oil
1 Murray cod fillet, skin on and cut
into 180g chunks
4 tablespoons tapenade (black olive paste)
150g spinach, cleaned and trimmed
50g butter
1/4 cup finely grated parmesan
1/4 cup toasted pine nuts
1/4 cup sultanas
salt and pepper

Heat some olive oil in a skillet and sear the cod
pieces, skin side down. Roast in a 250°C oven for
about 8-10 minutes – the cod should still be
opaque in the middle. Spread a little of the
tapenade thinly on the skin side of the cod, then
rest. Blanch the spinach in boiling water for about
1 minute. Drain well and place in a large, warm
bowl. Throw the butter, parmesan, pine nuts and
sultanas onto the spinach as soon as possible
while it is at its hottest. Mix well, season to taste
and serve immediately with the cod.

CAPONATA OF DEEP-SEA SCHNAPPER

Serves 6 as a main course

300g eggplant, cut into 1 cm dice
extra virgin olive oil
30g onion, cut into 1 cm dice
80g celery heart, cut into 1 cm dice
1 tablespoon sugar
2 tablespoons red wine vinegar
1 tablespoon pine nuts
50g Ligurian olives, pitted and chopped
50g tomato dice
20g Sicilian capers, washed and desalted
salt and pepper
160-180g schnapper per serve, cut into pieces

*Note: The proportions listed here are given only
as a guide – there is no substitute for taste.*

Pan-fry the eggplant in a little olive oil until it is
golden. Pan-fry the onion in a little olive oil as
well but do not let it colour. Blanch the celery for
2 minutes in boiling salted water. Lightly
caramelise the sugar, then add the vinegar to
make a syrup. Combine the syrup with the cooked
vegetables and the pine nuts, olives, tomatoes and
capers and mix thoroughly. Add a little extra virgin
olive oil, season to taste and mix again. Heat a
little olive oil in a pan, toss in the schnapper
pieces and fry until just done. Serve the caponata
warm with the fish pieces scattered throughout.

ROAST MURRAY COD WITH SPINACH, SULTANAS AND PINE NUTS

ROAST GUINEA FOWL WITH ROAST FENNEL AND PORCINI MUSHROOMS

Serves 12 as a main course

For the fennel

6 fennel bulbs, trimmed and cut into quarters
100g grated parmesan
salt and pepper
6 tablespoons extra virgin olive oil

Simmer the fennel in water only until the pieces have softened; do not overcook. Drain and allow to cool. Fill the folds of the fennel with the grated parmesan, season each quarter to taste and place on a roasting tray that has been brushed with the olive oil. Roast at 180°C until the faces of the fennel quarters are golden, 7-8 minutes.

For the sauce

50g dried porcini
180 ml red wine reduction (see recipe this page)
180 ml veal stock (see recipe this page)
salt and pepper

Soak the porcini in cold water until they are rehydrated. Heat the red wine reduction and the veal stock in a saucepan. When simmering, add the porcini mushrooms and cook for 10 minutes before serving. Season if necessary.

For the guinea fowl

Ingredients serve 12
6 x guinea fowls
salt

To prepare the guinea fowls, season the skin with a little salt. Place the guinea fowls in a roasting pan and roast in a preheated 250°C oven for 15-20 minutes. Serve with some of the porcini sauce and the roast fennel on the side.

VEAL STOCK

Makes 1 litre

3 kg veal bones, lightly roasted to give colour (about 30 minutes at 150°C)
4 onions, peeled and halved
3 leeks, cleaned and cut into large pieces
2 carrots, peeled and cut into large chunks
3 sticks celery, cleaned and cut into large chunks
4 cloves garlic, whole

Place all ingredients into a large stock pot and cover with fresh, cold water. Bring to a simmer and keep simmering for 8 hours. Strain the liquid into a large bowl. Place in the refrigerator overnight. The fat will rise to the top and solidify. In the morning it can be scooped off easily. Reduce the remaining stock until one litre remains. For a veal demiglace reduce the stock by half to two-thirds.

RED WINE REDUCTION

Makes 1 cup

1 onion, peeled and chopped
1 stick celery, cleaned and chopped
10 cloves garlic, peeled and chopped
3 tablespoons olive oil
1 cup balsamic vinegar
1.5 litres red wine

Lightly fry the onion, celery,and garlic in olive oil until they have wilted. Do not let them colour. Add the balsamic vinegar and reduce by three-quarters. Add the wine and reduce by half, skimming off any scum that gathers on the surface. Strain through muslin then reduce to 1 cup. The red wine sauce is then ready to use.

GRILLED LONG-TAILED BUGS WITH CANNELLINI BEANS AND OLIVE OIL, TOMATO AND SAFFRON SAUCE

VEAL TONGUE WITH GRILLED SWEET ONIONS AND FENNEL

Serves 4-6 as a main course

2–3 veal tongues according to size
1 carrot, roughly cut
1 onion, roughly cut
1 stick celery, roughly cut
$1/2$ cup wine vinegar
6 medium onions, extra, cut in half lengthways, skin left on
2 teaspoons cayenne
2 teaspoons paprika
1 tablespoon fennel seeds
salt and pepper
6 tablespoons extra virgin olive oil
250g green beans, blanched
1 cup rocket leaves
2 tablespoons chopped dried tomatoes
olive oil, extra
balsamic vinegar

Place the tongues, roughly cut carrot, onion, celery and the wine vinegar in a pot that is large enough to hold everything comfortably. Cover with cold water and bring to the boil. Turn the heat down to a simmer and cover the pot with a tight-fitting lid. The tongues will take anything from 45 minutes upward to cook. To tell if they are ready, prod the thick end of the tongues with a sharp knife; if the meat is done it will be tender but still firm. The tough outer skin of the tongues should peel easily when cooked. Keep the peeled tongues in their cooking liquid in a bowl. As long as they are completely covered by the liquid they will keep for a long time in the refrigerator.

Sprinkle the cut sides of the extra onions with the cayenne, paprika and fennel seeds. Season with salt and pepper and sprinkle with the olive oil. Place face down in a baking dish and roast at 190°C for 15 minutes until soft and brown. Peel the onions and add to a composite salad of the sliced tongue, beans and rocket. Dress with the dried tomatoes, olive oil and balsamic vinegar and serve.

GRILLED LONG-TAILED BUGS WITH CANNELLINI BEANS AND OLIVE OIL, TOMATO AND SAFFRON SAUCE

Serves 4 as a main course

For the sauce

2 kg ripe Roma tomatoes, peeled and mashed in a blender
pinch saffron
$1/2$ cup extra virgin olive oil
salt and pepper

Sieve the mashed tomatoes then place them in a pot with the saffron. Heat the purée until it is almost boiling. Remove from the heat and whisk in the olive oil a little at a time until it is well incorporated. Season to taste and allow to cool before using.

To serve

1 cup dried cannellini beans, soaked overnight
20 long-tailed bugs or Moreton Bay bugs
olive oil
4 tablespoons pesto (see recipe page 33)

Cook the beans in boiling salted water until 'al dente'. Drain and set them aside. Take the bug tails out of their shells carefully using sharp kitchen shears. Rub olive oil over each tail and grill them, making sure they don't dry out or go crusty; they should be golden and moist.
Heat the sauce and ladle a little onto each plate. Spoon some beans in, pile 4 or 5 bugs in the middle and finish each dish with a spoon of pesto.

ROSEWATER, STRAWBERRY, MERINGUE AND MASCARPONE TORTA

Serves 10

For the sponge

1 cup caster sugar
80 ml water
6 eggs, separated
1/2 cup plain flour
1/2 cup cornflour
1 teaspoon baking powder

Boil sugar and water together until soft ball stage is reached (use a sugar thermometer if you are unsure). Whisk the egg whites until soft peaks form, then gradually add the sugar syrup to the meringue, whisking continuously. Add the egg yolks, one at a time, and mix. Fold in the dry ingredients and combine well. Butter and flour 10 timbale moulds. Fill to two-thirds full with the mixture. Bake in a preheated 170°C oven for 10-15 minutes.

For the rosewater syrup

500g sugar
500 ml water
3 vanilla beans
2 oranges (zest only)
2 lemons (zest only)
2 limes (zest only)
1 bunch red roses (organic)

Boil together the sugar, water, vanilla beans and rinds until soft ball stage is reached.
Remove from the heat and add most of the rose petals, reserving some to use when serving.
Let the ingredients infuse together until cold.

For the Italian meringue

360g caster sugar
30g liquid glucose
80 ml water
6 egg whites

Boil together the sugar, glucose and water until it reaches about 110°C. Whisk the egg whites until soft peaks form. Gradually pour the sugar and glucose syrup into the egg whites, whisking continually until it has cooled. Pipe meringues 6 cm long and 2 cm wide onto silicone paper or baking sheets. Place on an oven tray and bake in a preheated 80°C oven until hard. This should take about 1 1/2 hours.

For the macerated strawberries

2 punnets of large strawberries
3 nips of Frangelico liquor
50 ml sugar syrup (made by dissolving 25g sugar in 25 ml water)

Dice the strawberries, mix into the liquor and sugar syrup. Macerate for a couple of hours.

For the oven dried strawberries

3 punnets of large strawberries
500 ml sugar syrup (made by dissolving 250g sugar in 250 ml water)

Thinly slice strawberries lengthwise, put into a bowl with sugar syrup. Mix well without breaking the strawberries. Layer them close together on an oven drying mat, put into the oven for 3 hours at the lowest temperature. Remove and put into an airtight container and refrigerate.

For the mascarpone

1 kg softened mascarpone

To assemble

Using a knife make a cavity in each of the sponge timbales and fill it with macerated strawberries. Cover the whole timbale with mascarpone. Sprinkle with pieces of the Italian meringue and encrust with oven dried strawberries on the top. Drizzle with the rosewater syrup all around the torta. Use the reserved fresh rose petals for decoration.

ROSEWATER, STRAWBERRY, MERINGUE AND MASCARPONE TORTA

ROAST NECTARINE, VANILLA AND RICOTTA TART

Serves 12

For the vanilla custard

1 litre pouring cream
1 vanilla bean, seeds scraped
20 egg yolks
180g caster sugar

Bring the cream and vanilla bean seeds to the boil. Cream the egg yolks and sugar, then pour the cream onto the yolks. Mix well, and cook over a low heat until very thick, stirring constantly. Strain and set in the refrigerator.

For the sweet short paste

500g plain flour
250g unsalted butter
200g icing sugar
1 egg
1 tablespoon vanilla essence

Blend the flour, butter and sugar until the butter coats the flour. Add the egg and vanilla essence until it all comes together in a ball. Rest overnight. Roll onto 12 tart cases and rest for 2-3 hours before baking. Bake blind in a preheated 180°C oven for 6-8 minutes or until a pale gold colour.

For the nectarines

6 nectarines, halved
500g brown sugar
1 quill cinnamon, freshly ground
125g butter
150 g dry ricotta

Place the nectarines facing up on a baking tray. Generously coat each nectarine with brown sugar and sprinkle over the cinnamon. Place a chunk of butter on each half. Bake in a 170°C oven for 5-8 minutes depending on their ripeness. Reserve the cooking liquid. Make small patties of ricotta and place on the bottom of each baked tart shell. Put 3 tablespoons of vanilla custard in each shell and top with a nectarine half. Drizzle the reserved cooking liquid from the nectarines around the tart.

CARAMEL, CHESTNUT, PINEAPPLE AND MASCARPONE ROTOLO

Serves 6-8

6 eggs, separated
75g caster sugar
150g caster sugar, extra
80g plain flour
100g icing sugar
400g mascarpone
100 ml thick caramel sauce
100g chestnuts, baked in a very hot oven,
peeled and crushed
1 pineapple

Cream the egg yolks and the caster sugar until thick and fluffy. Whip the egg whites and the extra caster sugar until they form soft peaks. Fold the two mixtures and the flour together. Spread onto a long, flat tray to about 2 cm in depth and bake in a preheated 170°C oven until just cooked. When cool, sprinkle with icing sugar. Mix the mascarpone and caramel sauce together. Spread onto the white side of the sponge (not the golden brown side). Sprinkle with the crushed chestnuts. Cut the core out of the pineapple and peel thoroughly. Thinly slice the pineapple and strain off any excess juices. Scatter the pineapple over the sponge. Roll up and dust with icing sugar. Rest overnight so that all the flavours combine. Cut with a serrated knife to serve.

CHERRIES 'SANTA LUCIA' WITH LEMONGRASS SORBETTO AND VANILLA GELATO

Serves 4

Vanilla gelato

160g sugar
8 egg yolks
1 vanilla bean, sliced lengthways
1 litre cream

Beat the sugar and egg yolks together until pale. Scrape the vanilla bean into the cream and heat until almost boiling. Whisk into the egg-sugar mixture. Cook over a low heat, stirring continuously with a wooden spoon until the mixture thickens and coats the spoon. Cool completely before churning.

Lemongrass sorbetto

4 sticks lemongrass, thinly chopped
1 litre sugar syrup (made from 500g sugar dissolved in 500 ml water)
1 litre lemon juice

Steep the lemongrass in the hot sugar syrup. Allow to cool and stand for 12 hours in the refrigerator. Add the lemon juice, strain out the lemongrass then churn.

Santa Lucia crumbs

125g plain flour
80g fine polenta flour
80g sugar
100g almond meal
grated zest of 1 lemon
80g butter, melted
100 ml duck or goose fat, melted
1 teaspoon vanilla essence
2 tablespoons grappa

Preheat the oven to 150°C. Sift the flour and combine with the dry ingredients.
Add the remaining ingredients and mix thoroughly by rubbing the mixture between the palms.
Lay the crumbs on flat trays and bake for 40 minutes, then lower the temperature to 80°C and bake for 2-3 hours until the crumbs have firmed and dried. Remove from the oven and allow to cool.

To assemble

1 litre dry red wine
1 tablespoon honey
1 quill cinnamon
pinch each cloves, peppercorns and star anise
1 vanilla bean, halved
zest and juice of 1 lemon and 1 orange
500g cherries, pitted

Place all of the ingredients except the cherries in a saucepan and over a simmering heat reduce by about half. Strain all the spices from the liquid, add the cherries, then bring the mixture back to the boil. Remove the cherries from the liquid, allow to cool, then store the cherries in the juice. To serve, spoon some cherries and some liquid on a plate, sprinkle on some Santa Lucia crumbs, add some vanilla gelato and lemongrass sorbetto and finally some more crumbs.

GOAT'S MILK PANNACOTTA WITH FRESH AND DRIED MANGO SALAD AND CHAMPAGNE JELLY

GOAT'S MILK PANNACOTTA WITH FRESH AND DRIED MANGO SALAD AND CHAMPAGNE JELLY

Makes 24

For the champagne jelly
500 ml champagne
sugar
3 gelatine leaves, soaked in cold water

Bring the champagne to the boil and add sugar to taste. Add the soaked gelatine leaves to the hot liquid. Pour the contents into a small container and chill.

For the goat's milk pannacotta
1.5 litres goat's milk
18 egg yolks
350g sugar
7 gelatine leaves, soaked in cold water
750g cream, whipped
fresh and dried mango

Bring milk to the boil. In a separate bowl, whisk together the egg yolks and sugar until pale in colour. Add the hot milk and combine well. Return to the stove and stir continuously until the custard coats the back of the spoon. Pour back into the original bowl. Squeeze out the excess water from the gelatine leaves and add to the custard. Stir well. Cool in the refrigerator. Once slight setting occurs, add the whipped cream and mix well. Place the mixture into small moulds.

Turn out the pannacotta into the centre of a plate, place chunks of fresh mango around and sprinkle with finely sliced and shredded dried mango. With a fork, break down the champagne jelly and spoon over the fruit.

HAZELNUT AND MASCARPONE TORTA

Serves 8-10

For the sponge
6 eggs, separated
75g caster sugar
150g caster sugar, extra
80g plain flour

Cream together the egg yolks and caster sugar until thick and fluffy. Whisk the egg whites and extra caster sugar until they form soft peaks. Fold the two mixtures and the sifted flour together. Spread into two rectangular baking trays and bake in a preheated 180°C oven until just undercooked.

For the soaking syrup
200 ml Frangelico liqueur
200 ml milk
80 ml sugar syrup (made from 50g sugar dissolved in 50 ml water)

Combine all of the ingredients and mix well.

For the filling
2 egg whites
50g caster sugar
1 kg mascarpone
150g roasted hazelnuts, chopped

Whisk the egg whites and sugar together until quite stiff. Fold into the mascarpone. The hazelnuts are used when assembling.

For the vanilla and hazelnut anglaise
2 vanilla beans
500 ml fresh cream
500 ml milk
200g caster sugar
8 egg yolks
2 teaspoons hazelnut paste

Place the vanilla beans, cream and milk in a saucepan and bring to the boil. Cream together the sugar and egg yolks until they form a ribbon. Whisk the mixture into the hot cream. Cook in a bain marie (or in a bowl set over a pot of boiling water), or on a low heat (80°C) until the custard thickens, stirring all the time. Slowly mix the hazelnut paste with the hot anglaise until well combined. Cool.

To assemble
Cut one of the sponges in half lengthwise, making sure it is even. Soak the bottom half in the soaking syrup just enough to moisten. Spread some of the mascarpone filling on the moistened sponge. Sprinkle with the roasted hazelnuts and cover with the top half of the sponge. Repeat this with the other sponge, reserving some hazelnuts for serving. To serve, cut into wedges, drizzle the anglaise around and sprinkle with hazelnuts.

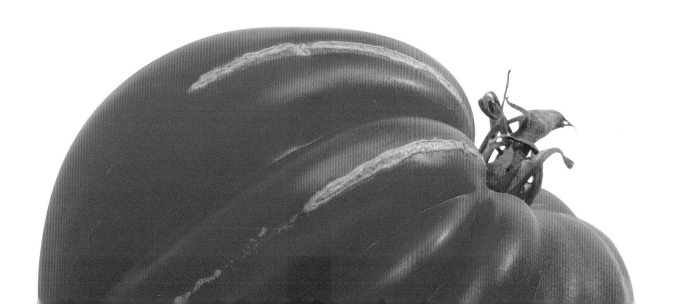

"YOU INHERIT STRUCTURES,

2

FORM

AND YOU HAVE TO WORK WITH THOSE." LUIGI ROSSELLI

...THE RESTAURANT CRITIC WAS A PERSON TO BE FEARED, REVERED AND OBEYED...

As a punter uses the form to back a winner, the 'restauranter' (a habitual and knowledgeable user of restaurants) uses the critics. In times past, the almost total reliance on the critic was both amusing and frightening.

In the 1970s, and to a lesser extent in the 80s, during the process of dining out democratisation in the New World, when we were learning to eat out comfortably, the restaurant critic was a person to be feared, revered and obeyed: a Petronius of the pots and pans, a dictator in the dining room. Such a personage in Sydney was Leo Schofield.

Schofield was, very properly, a legend in his own lunch and dinner time, a restaurant critic dragged through the courts for daring to suggest that a lobster was charred, whose approval could fill the house, whose downcast thumb could close the doors.

We remember clearly our first review from Leo Schofield in the mid 1980s. It was not just favourable, but highly complimentary. Later, Stefano described the ensuing stampede into the dining room as a 'shark feeding frenzy'. There was Leo's legion of loyal readers, seated patiently at table, his creased column open, desiring only to eat exactly as the great man had eaten. The problem was (on the first night anyway) our entire menu had changed completely, leaving most people a little puzzled as to what to order.

In those days, with little or no experience or discernment of their own to guide them, these new diners trusted the pronouncements of the critic without question. Schofield was absolutely essential to the dining out adolescence of this city. He taught diners to have standards and, in pointing out their shortcomings, forced restaurateurs grown lazy in an uncritical atmosphere to lift their games.

The form is not so crucial today, as we are far better educated. A bad review can no longer close a restaurant any more than a good one (as we noted at the time of our first dose of Leonine praise) can raise the revenue in a restaurant between 25 and 50 per cent of turnover for the five weeks following the review.

Today's diner will note a review, and perhaps decide to put the well reviewed on a list for a later visit and balance the badly reviewed against his or her own experience. Restaurants of better than average quality have proliferated to the point where one that is extravagantly praised will not affect the custom of the others. And the bad review will be judged based upon the reader's view of the reviewer, and the restaurant. No longer can we be brow-beaten by a reviewer's opinion. We have our own. And that has changed the form of relations between the diner and the restaurateur. ■

There is no such thing as a perfect restaurant, though there is the perfect restaurant experience. When all the variables come together, a great restaurant experience can deliver us onto another plane of existence. It can be very moving in much the same way as great theatre, music or art. Of course, like all performances, each one is different and I would be suspicious of any restaurateur who declared all services perfect.

I recall some time back a restaurant critic giving a restaurant a perfect 20 out of 20 on his personal marking scale. We all felt for the restaurateurs involved. On the one hand, a very favourable review is undoubtedly good for business – and ultimately, we have to stay in business, review or not. But the other side of the coin is a feeling of embarrassment because deep down, we know our peers and our competition very well, in many ways more intimately than the critic.

We all know who is using the highest quality ingredients. We know who has experienced staff and we know who is cutting corners. We also know to a large extent how well each of us run our restaurants. This is the nature of such a fashionable, fickle business.

Consequently restaurateurs know if they belong to the elite – the cream of the crop. They know because they are customer focused: they don't cut corners; they train their staff to the highest standards; their investment in scrupulously maintaining their restaurant is constant; the produce and the craft with which it is transformed and served is of the highest quality; and their cuisine has a cultural and philosophical resonance within their market. There is, therefore, a sense of injustice in being placed arbitrarily above one's peers, even if that injustice is mixed with such great publicity.

I remember some years ago, when I was writing a regular newspaper column, I'd been invited to dine with an internationally known food critic and author. We were four at the table and the critic was judging

the Sydney leg of 'Australia's Best Restaurant'. Our assigned waiter could only be described as incompetent; he was an embarrassment to the restaurant and to his profession. Not only did he make very basic mistakes, he also crossed the familiarity line in the sand, becoming very annoying.

We all knew he ruined the entire night and I felt deeply embarrassed for the owner and chef of the restaurant, who had produced a remarkable meal. To our amazement the guest critic, on whose opinion the award was given, said in a rather matter-of-fact manner, 'It's fortunate for this restaurant that I'm judging food and not service.' That particular restaurant won 'Australia's Best Restaurant' in that year.

The point is that the public and the restaurant community don't really know the critic's judging criteria or agenda. To one, food is most important. To another, ambience and service may be overriding factors.

To yet another, there may be the question of a close relationship with the restaurateur.

Newspaper editors have been known to employ their critics on the basis of controversy. Controversy, some have felt, sells papers. Therefore controversy is important to some critics.

Are critics essential? Like all reasonable people, I would defend the right to personal opinion. Every mature city needs intelligent critics who are able to make informed comment and venture opinions on subjects such as film, opera, theatre and all manner of performance, but it is the food critic who has to pass judgment on restaurants.

Food as performance is different to all other theatre because not only do we get the visual, the sound, the feel and even the smell, we also get to eat and taste the thing at the end. The whole experience literally passes through us. This is why we like to eat out and it is for this reason that we need good restaurant critics.

While the critics help us to make up our minds about where to go next, their opinions should be scrutinised against personal experience and trusted anecdote. Bearing that in mind, there are certain qualities in a critic's writing that I look for.

–The critic should be entertaining. Without a good grasp of the writing craft, there is no way a reader's attention can be held and the message communicated.

–A critic should be ethical and open and declare all conflicts of interest, both personal and financial. This fairly standard journalistic practice is overlooked quite often in the food media.

–The critic must be knowledgeable and informed on the subject, should research thoroughly and have both a historical and cultural perspective. Context is vitally important.

–The critic is not the subject. Though personal experience is fundamental in criticism, there is nothing more annoying than the critic that makes themself the subject.

Criticism should be read with scepticism and enjoyed for what it is – one person's opinion. This opinion should be filed in the mind and recalled when personal experience needs to be checked and measured. The restaurant experience is very personal and diversity is what makes a great city so exciting to live in. ■

STEFANO MANFREDI

"IT WAS TEN MONTHS BEFORE I THREW MY FIRST CUSTOMER OUT, BUT I WAS LIKE A SERIAL KILLER: ONCE I GOT THE TASTE FOR IT, I COULDN'T STOP. ON OUR BEST NIGHT, WE CHUCKED OUT 54 CUSTOMERS."

MARCO PIERRE WHITE

A waiter is suddenly at their side. 'One of you wanted an order of the bouillabaise stir fry?' he asks.

'Oh, God. What jerks,' says Liz. Matthew has the fleeting impression she's about to cry.

'We did order it, but I cancelled the order,' says Matthew. The waiter stands there looking at him with no expression.

Is he thinking this over? Is he going to come to some decision, or is he paralyzed in the face of a novel situation?

'You don't want it then?' asks the waiter.

Matthew almost laughs. Liz explodes. 'Of course we don't want it. That's why we cancelled it. We only ordered it because we couldn't eat *this* crap.'

'Was there something you disliked about the squid-ink pasta?'

'There was a great deal we didn't like about the squid-ink pasta,' says Liz with a sneer she'd like to turn on Matthew. 'It was too peppery, for one thing. You shouldn't put so much pepper on a dish like this. I've had this dish in many restaurants, including restaurants in Italy –'

She has? When?

' – and it's never as peppery as this.'

She likes spicy food. This isn't about the food. This is about me.

FROM *RESERVATIONS RECOMMENDED* BY ERIC KRAFT

This excerpt from Eric Kraft's brilliant comedy of modern New York manners could and should be used in hotel management schools to train waiters. It exhibits many facets of the complex relationship between diner and waiter (in dismissing 'waiternoia' we don't deny that the relationship is complex). The waiter, poor soul, is the easily slappable face of the restaurant – especially in the way that the waiter in the piece delivers the worst kind of 'robotic' service.

In this excerpt, Matthew (in reality the feared and revered restaurant critic B.W. Beath) is dining with his ex-wife. It is an extreme example of the difficulty of maintaining 'good form' between restaurant and diner. We see them every night, those who appear to have come to dinner either determined to have a bad time, or having domestic problems. Nothing we do will change their mind. The rules are very simple in a case like this: everything is our fault.
That is the first rule of being a restaurateur.

A meal came back into the kitchen; it was duck. The duck had been bitten into. The waiter holding the plate said, 'I'm really embarrassed at having to tell you this, but the lady says this is not duck, it's lamb.'

I wanted to understand what it was about this person that had made them do this. Were they arguing? The waiter said, no, the patron simply said, it's not duck, it's lamb. But I could see that it was a duck leg because, to dignify the argument with an observation, lambs aren't that little and they don't have that shape. But the whole thing, as a restaurateur, is that you have to please people, that's the guiding rule, even if the customer is completely ignorant, even if they come from Mars and don't know the difference between duck and lamb. And you must do it in a way that doesn't belittle them at all.

What I did was I went out. I was really busy, but I went out. And I asked her if she would like to order something else. She said no, so I told her that she had ordered the duck and I had cooked duck. She said well, I'll have it back. I said to her that I just wanted her to have a good time and that if there was anything I could do for her to please let the waiter know.

STEFANO MANFREDI

line from the movie *Wall Street* where upwardly mobile Bud is sitting in front of an impeccably prepared Japanese spread, saying to his friend, 'It's too perfect. Let's not eat. Let's just watch it and think about it.'

In that era, power shifted to the kitchen and the word from the kitchen was 'No!' Remember asking for salt, pepper or extra petit fours only to be told that the food is as the chef would like it seasoned and no, the petit fours were only for people who had ordered dessert before coffee? Remember the tantrums and the curt reply at being told that you couldn't have your fillet of beef cooked medium-well? If you were a good lip reader, a quick glance at the chef through the open kitchen would have caught the mouthing of the word 'Philistine' aimed in your direction.

Sydney, like New York, is very big on those brooms that sweep clean. Unlike more genteel cities where tradition lingers and change is gradual, Sydney turns the page, and moves on.

There has been, in the last ten years, a significant shift of power back to the patron/diner that has been caused by the adoption, by the best service providers (restaurants, hotels, stores), of a service policy based upon doing exactly what the customer wants. This service culture arose in the United States firstly as a competitive weapon – when all else is equal, service is the determinant of patronage – and has become deeply imbued in American culture. It is best expressed by the Neiman Marcus policy of directing staff to ask any complainant in any of their stores upon receipt of any complaint at all a simple question: 'What would you like me to do about it?' Such a service culture is beginning to make inroads in the more deeply Celtic (and, therefore, rebellious) Australian collective consciousness.

The 1980s saw the rise of the chef and the 'temple of gastronomy' which was fuelled by the 'greed is good' power-brokers of that decade. There is an apt

Some years ago, commentators in Australia and elsewhere were decrying the demise of Fine Dining. It was noted, when a restaurant called Oasis Seros closed in 1994, that it was one of many recipients of the Remy Martin *Gourmet Traveller* Magazine Restaurant Of The Year award to suffer the same fate. The death of fine dining and the rise of cafe culture and sloppy standards was predicted.

This has since been proven not to be the case. That rash of closures in the early to mid 1990s was, rather, the second in a series of corrections in the movement of restaurant culture in Sydney. The first of those closure corrections was the end of the 'Toffs Only' restaurant; in Sydney these were, in the 1940s, '50s and '60s, places like Kenneil in Kings Cross (an officers only restaurant during the war), Romano's in the city and Chelsea, also in Kings Cross. Every city had them. Dining out, in those times, was a class privilege. If you dared to wander into these mirrored and glistening corridors of culinary power and you didn't fit, heaven help you.

It was the democratisation of dining that killed off those restaurants, which were then replaced, at that level, by the Temples of Gastronomy, where the dictator chef ruled. The elite were happy at the Chelsea, the foodocrats were treated well at Oasis Seros.

The second of the cultural shifts killed off the Temples of Gastronomy. The dominant memory of dining in those 'fine dining' restaurants of the 1980s is of small, hushed rooms. We murmured. We ate mainly in silence. Was there a slight puritan edge to it? Were we still a little guilty at eating out? Did we feel that this was not our place, that there was something of the farmhand being invited into the manor house for the once a year dinner?

"WHEN YOU GO TO A RESTAURANT, AND YOUR EXPECTATIONS ARE MET, YOU WILL BE HAPPY. IF THEY'RE SURPASSED, YOU WILL BECOME A LOYAL CUSTOMER."

STEFANO MANFREDI

It was that period when restaurants seemed to be run by 15 year olds who 'invented' everything, who threw the classic out the window (duck, there goes Escoffier) and who then discovered that Australia was not in Europe but just below a big place called, collectively, Asia.

You remember it well. You discovered coriander in everything, whether you liked it or not. It was when a dish could (and did) appear on a menu described as 'Risotto of Japanese Scallops and Fresh Herbs with a Green Coconut Curry Sauce'.

Hand in glove with this period of culinary 'freedom' went the Age of Attitude. A waiter would sidle up to your table, inspect you to see if you fit, and then ask if you wanted anything. Pity the poor diner who had a question. 'You've never heard of brandade?' It was a black period (literally, if you didn't wear black you weren't allowed into the highest gastro temples) and it is, thankfully, over.

Now, once again, Sydney is a wonderful place to eat. What happened? Well, what always happens. We grew up. The smart young chefs looked around their restaurants and realised they might have been serving cutting edge food but that no one was there to eat it.

We have discovered a very simple notion: the total dining experience. First, we had to come to terms with the inescapable fact that restaurants are about more than eating; it's all very well to understand such a concept intellectually, it's another thing altogether to build it into the way you do business. Once that revelation is firmly embedded – and it is a big discovery for a city founded on cocky egalitarian ideals – we can admit that service is at least as important as food. One Very Important Chef recently told us of his own journey towards this conclusion. 'Do you realise,' he asked with a pained expression, 'how hard that is for a chef to admit?'

Meanwhile, in the kitchen, good sense is again prevailing. The young Turks have grown up and realised that there is more to cooking than stir fry and coriander. Many of them decided to learn technique. Suddenly, skills were seen as important.

But we have, thankfully, learnt to do it all – service, food and décor – our own way. Gone from the new world is any attempt at aping le style Français, which has been left way behind in the 1970s. As Sydney restaurant critic Terry Durack so correctly concluded, after a meal at Restaurant Alain Ducasse, 'We have nothing like it in Sydney, but then, we shouldn't even want anything like it. A three-star French restaurant is a very special part of a visit to France ...'

Now that so many of us can afford to dine out, and we know a lot more about food, the third wave is definitely upon us. First to go was the silver salver, and then, 10 or 15 years later, the sneering waiter. The contract is now between a more relaxed, much more knowledgeable service-oriented restaurant and chef, and a more knowledgeable and much more relaxed clientele. When a diner walks into a restaurant, they can do so in the knowledge that they will be treated well. The twin peaks of waiter hostility – sneering and fawning – should have been banished. If they're not, you're in the wrong place.

That's not to say that there are no 'Siberias' in Australian restaurants today, nor favoured tables. But what is lacking here is what Adam Gopnik wrote about, also in a New Yorker piece on modern French cooking: '... the endless worry in Los Angeles and New York about power tables – where you sit in Spago, what time you leave Four Seasons ...' is not such a big deal in Australia. If you can afford the price of entry, once you're in, there is little discrimination in the real sense. At bel mondo, for example, one of the most favoured tables in the house is 40. It is not owned by anyone, merely desired by many. If you want it, all you have to do is book far enough ahead to get it.

But with diner's rights go diner's responsibility. There is now an implicit contract signed between diner and restaurateur as soon as you walk through that door and sit in that seat. The restaurateur's part of the bargain is the delivery of food, service and a good experience. The diner, for his or her part, agrees to accept these services, dishes and experiences with grace, and to pay for them – unless there is a serious breach of the agreement. How these breaches are dealt with is an occasion for the display of diner good form.

bel mondo had been open for six months and in that time we received quite a large amount of feedback – most of it positive, mind you, with the occasional complaint, with justification, from guests who had had less than a great experience. These complaints are inevitable in a restaurant, especially one as large and high profile as *bel mondo*, and the way they are handled is important to the development of our service and the way we train our staff.

JULIE MANFREDI-HUGHES

There are, basically, three ways of making your displeasure known in a restaurant. The first is to complain calmly and clearly. Explain what is wrong and why you think it is wrong. The difficulty here is that you may not know why it is wrong, just that you don't like it. If, for example, you have tried, say, sweetbreads for the first time and genuinely don't like them, we applaud your courage and will replace them. If, on the other hand, the meat that is delivered is not cooked to your instructions, that is easy. Tell us what you want. Ask for it.

Remember that a good restaurateur is delighted to receive constructive criticism. Feedback is crucial to continued development.

The second method of complaining is to write a letter. We're not great fans of the letter after the event. The meal has usually gone, as has the moment, and details are blurred by time. There are occasions when a letter is appropriate, but the instant qualified complaint is preferred. We remember being terribly impressed, having been taken to a very fine restaurant in Paris in the 1970s by one who was a regular patron of that restaurant, by the way a complaint was handled. The first courses had arrived, and our host had a problem with his. He raised his hand, the maître d' arrived and they conferred quietly. The maître d' straightened up and clicked his fingers, the waiters appeared, whisked away our first course plates, and handed out menus. Please re-order Mesdames and Messieurs, the entire meal is compliments of the house. Baboom.

The third method of complaining is to sit, stewing, say nothing, leave and never come back. At times, we know, there is no point in complaining. It is often pointless in a restaurant where it is quite obvious they just don't 'get it'. But in a good restaurant, this makes no sense. We can see that you are unhappy, and that makes us unhappy, and nothing gets any better from then on.

And how do you show your pleasure? By telling us what you enjoyed and why you enjoyed it. Restaurateurs are no different to anyone else: we thrive on praise. ∎

Perhaps the most important aspect of form is the design, shape and space of the restaurant. When Stefano wrote in the preface to his book *Fresh From Italy* that 'the new cannot exist without the traditional, and that tradition is constantly being nourished by the new', he was referring specifically to food. When the restaurant moved from a back lane in Ultimo to the top floor of the 1913 Argyle Department Store (originally the Cleland Store) in the Argyle Bond Stores complex in Sydney's Rocks area, it took on a broader prophetic meaning.

The move was not without difficulty for us or our architect, Luigi Rosselli, particularly at that point where the commercial requirements of designing and installing a restaurant in a Heritage building cautiously protected by the Sydney Cove Authority met: there was some dissension at the interface of history and commerce.

But what was most interesting was the way in which the solutions to these problems – as well as the site itself – reinforced some of the not quite so old traditions of the restaurant over which the family had presided for the past 13 years.

The Restaurant in Hackett Street, Ultimo was one of the first Sydney restaurants to offer diners a view into the kitchen, transforming that room from a mysterious source of delicious smells and clanging sounds behind a swinging door to a stage for its players, the chefs. But by 1995, now trading as The Restaurant Manfredi, it had obviously outgrown its small (75 seat), eccentric location.

"WHEN LEIGH PRENTICE, ARCHITECT AND RESTAURANT DESIGNER, APPROACHES A RESTAURANT DESIGN, HE LOOKS AT THE ROOM, THE CHAIR, AND THE FOOD. IN THAT ORDER. COME TO THINK OF IT, THAT'S THE WAY YOU ENGAGE WITH A RESTAURANT."

JOHN NEWTON

In September 1995, we found and secured the Argyle Store space and engaged architect Luigi Rosselli, who inspected the site and produced rough plans. In August 1996, work began. That nine month gap was filled with protracted negotiations between the Manfredi camp and the Sydney Cove Authority.

Restaurant design, as those of you who have attempted it will know, is a curious discipline. A restaurant is a convivial public space. Rosselli believes that in Sydney it is — along with the beach — 'the public space — you don't have a square to stroll in like Italy, and you don't go to church and meet everyone like in an American country town. Sydney is a hedonistic town, we like to be comfortable and our body and our stomachs are a part of it.'

Rosselli, who has designed some of Sydney's most significant recent restaurants and cafes (Cicada, Verona, La Mensa, Vault), also points out that one of the major restrictions is that mostly 'you inherit structures, and you have to work with those'. In this instance, in addition to a practically inviolable structure, he inherited the interventions of another architect. Lifts, connecting stairways and other details had been incorporated by Allen Jack and Cottier. Rosselli pays tribute to them. 'They've done beautiful work ... they have recognised the original function of the building.'

In the instance of *bel mondo*, Rosselli said, 'We were working with a beautiful building — the simplicity of a strong warehouse, big beams, columns and piers, it's the beauty of an old commercial building, very hard to attain with a new structure.'

The principles with which Rosselli begins design are light, space, sound and the texture of the materials. 'At *bel mondo* we had a very limited scope in that we could not work on the existing structure due to heritage requirements — we couldn't even paint the walls. So we positioned major elements like the kitchen and the bar like furniture.'

Both the bar and a large sweeping wall leading to the kitchen were clad in rusting mild steel plate, the colour echoing both Italy (umber) and the outback (ochre) and collaborating with the rough-hewn industrial nature of the Allen Jack & Cottier interventions.

Rosselli broke up the large space (around 400 square metres) into several smaller ones, partly in line with our brief, partly to bring it down to a smaller scale so as to be 'different from those large eating areas in London, where you feel there's a factory production of food — here you feel the food is more artisanal, in keeping with the family'.

The first thing you see on entering is the Antibar, a long, sinuous stainless steel topped curve, that defines while leading into the formal restaurant, a space at once comfortable and dramatic. Behind the Antibar nestles the Antibar eating area, more informal, no bookings, stone top tables, plates of antipasto, wines by the glass, drinks from the bar. And beyond that, the main dining room, the ranks of white clothed tables topped by dim, glowing table lamps. Beyond that, intriguing views over the western rooftops to The Rocks ('Block out the bridge and it's Glasgow,' said Rosselli) and east to the harbour and the Opera House.

There is one serendipitous result of the clash between conservation and occupation. The Heritage strictures on interfering with the floor also meant that the plumbing could not go beneath it, so that the entire kitchen had to be raised and is even more of a stage than in the old restaurant. Rosselli comments, 'It is an asset [for Steve]. He's a pretty public person, he likes working in an open kitchen, and being raised will be even more theatrical.'

A strange fit — between old Italian and Modern Australian — in a warehouse. Like putting an Armani suit on a lifesaver? 'No,' says Rosselli, 'Armani is the stereotype of Italian fashion. I wouldn't think of Manfredi's as stereotype Italian cuisine. We're nothing to do with Italian architecture here. What is "Manfredi" here is the theatrical nature of the design.'

And here is the essence of the success of this — and other — Rosselli restaurant designs. He is no dictator. He works with the restaurateur to achieve the final design. He gets to know them, understand them, and translates that knowledge of who his clients are into a restaurant of his own design. 'You must be inquisitive, not self centred, you have to listen very carefully to what the client wants, to understand the client.'

BEL MONDO MOMENTS

THE ROCK STAR

We were visited midweek by a well known rock star who was touring Australia quite successfully due, in no small part, to the media frenzy whipped up by naive parents who were protesting to their local member of parliament about the effects of satanic lyrics, allegedly contained in his songs, on their children. He came to *bel mondo* with his girlfriend and a couple of assistants. They ordered well and chose interesting wines. His girlfriend had ordered the gnocchi with fresh black truffles, burnt butter and parmesan. As the waiter placed the gnocchi in front of her, she took a long whiff of their pungent aroma, turned to her boyfriend and said, 'Darling, they smell just like sperm!'

UN PESCE NON SI PUÓ FRIGGERE CON L'ACQUA.

» » »

Which is not to say that he does not have strong ideas of his own. 'I dislike [restaurant] architecture that has a masochistic edge for the people who use it. Places that hurt your ears or that are uncomfortable. The restaurant is a place for comfort.'

Commenting on the anomalies of introducing an Italian restaurant into an old Australian building, Julie said that for her it 'made perfect sense. What we do is all about the blending of the old and the new. Not just the place and the food, but the whole style, the presentation, the service. You couldn't do a restaurant like this anywhere else in Australia. I love the Italian restaurants in Melbourne with their dark wood and copper everywhere – but you walk outside and you see the misty river. Here in Sydney, it's much lighter. The thing I love most about this space is the warm sunny quality of the light, the views across the city's icons.'

Julie also chose the name. 'The day that Steve and I went in to first look at the space, the light was streaming in and it was this warm glowing timber clad space with the patina of age, and I went home that night and looked at the Ragazzini [*il Nuovo Ragazzini*, the Italian English dictionary] and I looked up the word fashion, because there was something about being in The Rocks and being on top of a retail development that made me think of the fashion element of what we do.

'I came upon the expression *"il bel mondo"*, which means the fashion set, fashionable society in Italy. We left the "il" aside, and ran with *bel mondo*. It's a simple name and it can mean many things to many people. It was meant to be ironic in that there was an aspect of it that came from the heart, an aspect that came from the intellect and another that came from having a sense of humour about the industry. I wanted it to reflect Sydney's relaxed sense of style – it's not high fashion, it's not stiff and it's not pretentious – I did not want to have a stiff and pretentious restaurant.'

When we opened, patrons of the old restaurant found much that was changed, and much that was not. It's still in a slightly out of the way position. The kitchen is even more of a performance space. But overall, thanks to a close relationship between architect and client, and in spite of what appears on the surface to be an incongruous setting, the spirit has survived the move unbroken. ■

IF THE PRODUCE IS NOT RIGHT A COOK CAN'T WORK.

Sally Hunter is a glass maker, whose dessert plates were the first of the commissioned pieces used in The Restaurant in 1985. Today, she works with us as product manager to develop a range of merchandise arising from the products – both food and utensils – that we use in the restaurant.

Restaurateurs in Australia have specific signatures. Some write books, some produce CDs. Some align themselves with the arts. The tendency of a restaurant to move away from just selling food on plates says a lot about our relationship with restaurants.

Restaurants have changed the way we eat in Australia, they've had a very important educative role to play. Going to restaurants has become a very important part of our lives. We're influenced, not just by the food, but by the surroundings, and the products used in them.

A restaurant like bel mondo has requirements for products, produce, wine, requirements which are continuously developing. It was a group of restaurateurs, for example – Stefano among them – who developed Illabo lamb. A range of products is a natural extension of that kind of creativity.

The Manfredis have always supported the arts and designers. So what I'm doing fits in perfectly in terms of dealing with artists and designers to develop products. But the products we develop have to have meaning. We can't just go and develop a funky range of saucepans. The design brief has to be written by Stefano or Franca or others in the kitchen. So it's a set of saucepans designed by professional cooks.

We're currently in the middle of a design exercise for new plates and coffee cups with a ceramic artist, Rod Banford. For me he's probably one of the most professional ceramicists in Australia. The restaurant opened with a terrific range from Gerry Wedd. His designs have given the restaurant a signature – it's fun, it's cheeky – now we are moving on to the next stage.

I began working with Rod on coffee cups, and then, after he'd met Stefano and Julie, who were impressed with his skills, we began working with him on plate design. Rod's plates will eventually replace the last of my own pieces.

But it's a long haul project. After we've agreed on the design, we have to line up a manufacturer – he'll want to make 200,000 minimum – then an agent, a distributor. There are a lot of planets that have to line up even to get one measly cup out.

Rod's been looking for this opportunity for some time. It's not one that comes up in Australia a lot. There's very little manufacturing here for artists and designers. They rarely get that mass manufacturing experience or opportunity.

This part of the business has to be self funding in the long term. We [the designers and the family] have to work together to get the project up in the short term. There's no guarantees, but we'll all benefit in the long term if these products get manufactured. It's the only way it can happen without an enormous amount of resources.

I'd predict that it'll be about five per cent of our business for the next five years. If that happened, we'd all be happy. But it's a slow process. I went to one of the International Trade Fairs and I saw maybe five pieces that have meaning. I don't think it's too ambitious for us to aim for that. We don't have to fill shelves. Just very slowly develop products within the framework of the restaurant. ■

SALLY HUNTER

Finally, another important element of form is that of food on the plate. The way food is placed on the plate at *bel mondo* has much to do, again, with the heritage in the kitchen.

'Maybe because my parents come from a rural town in the north of Italy, and on my father's side of the family they're peasants – in the European sense of farm workers – that I have an aversion to fussy overworked, over art directed food.

'I leave that sort of design to have fun with at the end of the meal, because dessert is much more precise, geometrically and scientifically – it's about as close to science as you can get in food.

'We have a liberal philosophy of plating. If it was, for example, a dish of beef and winter vegetables, I would say that the beef goes in the centre of the plate, and that the vegetables should be scattered, and then sauced. And that's it. That's the instruction. I particularly like, on a dish like that, to leave it to chance. Of course this all depends on the composition skills of the chef who's putting it together, and some are better than others.

'If you look at the definition of garnish in gastronomy, you'll see that it specifies accompaniments that are edible, not just displays. A mint sprig is not garnish, it is a mint sprig. I don't know where it came from – and the strawberry, and the parsley. It's just awful. Real garnishes are accompaniments and satellites that surround the main dish. They are dishes in their own right.

'In the strictest sense of the word, all cooks garnish their food. The vegetables that accompany the roast are a garnish. The salad, prepared to be eaten with the fish, is a garnish. A distinction needs to be made between the garnish and the decoration that occurs as an afterthought.

'I once worked with a chef who would place himself at a certain point in the kitchen where the dishes were plated, ready to be taken to the table by the waiters. It was the apprentice's job to make sure that little bowls full of sprigs of various herbs were always available, set out before him so that as a final artistic gesture he would place his signature on each dish that went out.

'I have a friend who believes that somewhere in the world there's a parsley farmer who sells curly parsley to restaurants that use it only for garnish. This farmer makes a fortune selling parsley that is destined never to be eaten.

'Having learnt to cook from my grandmother and my mother, the concept of decoration of the plate is quite foreign to my cooking. Those who love food know that honest food cooked from the best ingredients has a beauty that needs no other adornment. All that other stuff is distraction created by cooks with too much spare time on their hands.' ■

STEFANO MANFREDI

"GARNISH/GARNITURE: A SINGLE ITEM OR COMBINATION OF VARIOUS ITEMS ACCOMPANYING A DISH ... WHETHER SIMPLE OR COMPOSITE, THE GARNISH ALWAYS BLENDS WITH THE FLAVOUR OF THE BASIC DISH AND THE SAUCE (IF THERE IS ONE) ..."

LAROUSSE GASTRONOMIQUE

RECIPES

DEEP FRIED ZUCCHINI FLOWERS STUFFED WITH TASMANIAN GRUYERE

Serves 6 as a first course

200g plain flour
$^2/_3$ cup cold water
24 zucchini flowers, with baby zucchini attached
250g Heidi Tasmanian gruyère cheese, grated
olive oil
salt and pepper
salad greens

Mix together the flour and the water to make a rough lumpy batter. Set aside to rest while you prepare the rest of the dish. Trim the ends of the zucchinis. Now carefully open the ends of the flowers and fill them with a little grated cheese. Heat enough olive oil to deep fry the zucchini flowers. When the oil is about to smoke, dip the filled zucchini flowers in the batter, allowing any excess batter to run off. Fry the flowers in the oil until they are golden. Season to taste and serve with salad greens.

BEL MONDO'S GNOCCHI WITH BURNT BUTTER AND TRUFFLES

Serves 6–8 as a first course

1 $^1/_2$ kg potatoes (It is very important that you choose potatoes that do not retain a lot of moisture. Older potatoes are best so, generally speaking, choose potatoes that are not new season.)

plain flour
$^1/_2$ teaspoon grated nutmeg
150g parmesan, grated
salt
2 egg yolks
50g butter per serve
150g truffles, finely sliced

Cook the unpeeled potatoes in a little water, lid on, until they are cooked (thus virtually steaming them and limiting the amount of moisture they retain). Peel and mash them, preferably with a schiacciapatate, a ricer, mouli or a passaverdure and form a pile with a well in the middle that resembles a volcano. Do not put the potatoes in a blender.

For every kilogram of potatoes add a small handful of flour to the well in the potato. Then add the freshly grated nutmeg, a spoonful of parmesan, a pinch of salt and lastly the egg yolks. (The egg yolks are always added last so that they don't come in direct contact with the heat of the potato.) Fold the mixture together continually toward the centre, gradually adding more flour if necessary. (Remember that the more flour that is added, the firmer the gnocchi will be.) Once the potato mixture has come together, allow it to rest for 5 minutes. Take a little of the mixture and form it into a long sausage shape, 3 cm in diameter. With a knife, cut the sausage into 3 cm lengths. Form each dumpling by running it, with the thumb, along the back of the tines of a fork This is the perfect design for gnocchi. The ridges, from the fork, hold the sauce and the indent on the other side, formed by the thumb, helps it cook quickly and evenly.

To serve, poach the gnocchi in plenty of (not furiously) boiling salted water until they rise to the surface. Remove from the water and arrange on a plate. Meanwhile, place the butter in a small pot over a high heat until it has turned a nut brown colour. Turn off the heat and add the truffles to the burnt butter. Sprinkle the gnocchi with the remaining parmesan and spoon over the sizzling butter. Serve immediately.

SEARED TUNA WITH HERBS AND LEEKS AND FRESH HORSERADISH AND OLIVE OIL DRESSING

ASPARAGUS AND FONTINA PIZZETTA

Serves 8–10 as a first course

15g fresh yeast
250g plain flour
pinch salt
2 tablespoons olive oil
1 cup fresh tomato sauce (see recipe page 35)
1 1/2 cups grated Fontina cheese
40 asparagus spears, trimmed to fit the pizzetta
1/2 cup chopped herbs: thyme, rosemary, oregano
salt and pepper
4 cloves garlic, minced into 1/4 cup extra virgin olive oil

Dissolve the yeast in 750 ml tepid water. Make a well in the flour and mix in the dissolved yeast, salt and olive oil. Knead well until the dough is smooth and even. Place in a bowl, cover with a tea towel and allow to rise for about 30 minutes. Cut pieces from the main dough and, on a floured work surface, roll out discs, quite thin, giving a base about 15 cm in diameter. These can be done directly onto metal pizza moulds that have been lightly oiled. Spread 2 tablespoons of the tomato sauce on each base. Sprinkle some cheese over, followed by some asparagus and herbs. Season to taste and sprinkle on the garlic oil. Cook in a 250°C oven for 10 minutes. Serve immediately.

LAMB AND BORLOTTI BEAN FRITTATA

Serves 4 as a first course

200g borlotti beans, shelled
6 tablespoons extra virgin olive oil
parsley, chopped
salt and pepper
2 lamb loins, trimmed and left whole
4 whole eggs
1 tablespoon grated parmesan
6 dried tomatoes, finely chopped
tender rocket leaves

Place the borlotti beans in a saucepan, cover with water and bring to the boil. Reduce the heat and simmer for 15 minutes until the beans are tender. Drain off the cooking liquid and dress the beans with some of the olive oil and a handful of parsley. Season to taste. Mash half the beans with a fork until they form a textured purée.

Preheat the oven to 220°C. Heat some olive oil in a skillet and sear the lamb loins for about 20 seconds on each side. Roast in the oven for 8 minutes, then remove from the heat and rest for 10 minutes. Beat the eggs together in a bowl with the parmesan, dried tomatoes and salt and pepper. Heat some olive oil in a skillet, and when it begins to smoke, add the egg mixture, working it around the bottom of the pan so that it cooks evenly. This should take about 1 minute, and the surface should look creamy. Transfer to a plate, place the mashed borlotti mixture in a line in the centre of the frittata and roll the lot into a large cigar shape. Slice into sections and serve with the sliced lamb loin, the rocket and the rest of the whole beans.

LINGUINI WITH TASMANIAN BLACK MUSSELS AND TOMATO AND JERUSALEM ARTICHOKE SAUCE

Serves 6 as a first course

100 ml extra virgin olive oil
1 medium onion, diced small
300g Jerusalem artichokes, peeled and cut into 5 mm slices
4 cloves garlic, minced
200g ripe tomatoes, seeded, peeled and roughly chopped
10–12 basil leaves, torn into small pieces
36 live mussels, scrubbed, beards removed
salt and pepper
60–80g fresh linguini per person (see recipe below)

In a pan, heat half the olive oil and lightly fry the onion, Jerusalem artichokes and garlic for 2–3 minutes. Add the tomatoes and basil and simmer for 10 minutes until the artichokes are tender but not soft. Add the mussels and allow them to open, then add their juices to the sauce. Remove from the heat, season to taste and toss into the cooked pasta. Serve immediately.

For the linguini

Make a well in about 100g plain flour. Add enough whole eggs (it should take 1 or 2) so that when they are worked into the flour, the dough is not sticky and not dry. Compensate by adding more flour if too sticky, or more egg if too dry. Cut the pasta dough into smaller workable pieces so it can be easily passed through a pasta machine. Roll it until the pasta is smooth and silky. Pass the sheets through the linguini cutter and hang to dry a little. Cook the pasta in an abundant amount of rapidly boiling, salted water until 'al dente'. Drain the pasta and dress with some olive oil so that the strands don't stick to one another as they cool.

GRILLED COFFIN BAY SCALLOPS WITH SALSIFY, ROAST GARLIC AND PEAS

Serves 6 as a first course

2 whole bulbs garlic
$^1/_4$ cup extra virgin olive oil
salt and pepper
$^1/_2$ cup extra virgin olive oil for frying
1 medium-sized salsify, peeled and cut in julienne pieces (these can be stored in cold water until needed)
salt, extra
1 cup fresh peas, shelled and blanched
extra virgin olive oil, extra
3 dozen Coffin Bay scallops in the half shell, cleaned
3 cloves garlic, minced into $^1/_4$ cup extra virgin olive oil
3 tablespoons thyme, rosemary and parsley, finely chopped

Preheat the oven to 150°C. Place the garlic bulbs on a baking tray and roast in the oven for about 20–30 minutes or until they are soft and creamy inside. Allow to cool, then slice the bulbs in half across the cloves, and squeeze the garlic out into the bowl of a food processor. Add the olive oil, season to taste and pulse a few times to purée. Heat the frying oil in a high-sided frypan and fry the julienned salsify quickly for about 30 seconds until they colour slightly. Drain them on some absorbent paper and season with salt. Toss the peas in a little extra virgin olive oil and season with salt and pepper. Turn the oven up to 220°C, place the scallops on baking trays and sprinkle each with the olive oil and garlic mixture. Also sprinkle each with some of the chopped herbs, season and bake in the oven for 5–8 minutes. When done, serve with the garlic purée, the peas and the fried salsify.

PRAWN AND LEEK RAVIOLI

Serves 8 as a first course

2 kg king prawns, cooked, peeled and deveined (retain the heads and shells)
3 medium-sized leeks, cut into 5 mm thick rounds (retain the leek trimmings)
1 carrot, peeled and cut into 2 cm rounds
2 sticks celery
2 ripe tomatoes, chopped
3 cloves garlic, peeled and left whole
extra virgin olive oil
salt and pepper
500g basic pasta dough (see recipe this page)
100g butter

Place the prawn shells and heads in a stock pot with the leek trimmings, carrot, celery, tomatoes and garlic. Cover with water and bring to the boil. Turn down the heat and simmer for 1 hour. Strain and then reduce to about half a litre of concentrated stock.

Simmer the leek rounds in extra virgin olive oil until soft. Season to taste and allow to cool completely. Roll out the dough with a pasta machine to the desired thickness and cut out 6 cm squares. Place a prawn and some leek just off the middle of each square, keeping a little of the edge free. With a brush dipped in water, moisten the edges of the square, fold over gently and press lightly with your fingers, sealing the ravioli. Place the finished ravioli on a floured board ready to be cooked.

Bring the stock back to the boil, turn off the heat and whisk in the cold butter. Season with salt and pepper if necessary. Cook the ravioli in plenty of boiling salted water for a couple of minutes, drain and serve dressed with the sauce.

For the pasta dough

Make a well in about 100g plain flour. Add enough whole eggs (it should take 1 or 2) so that when they are worked into the flour, the dough is not sticky and not dry. Compensate by adding more flour if too sticky, or more egg if too dry. Cut the pasta dough into smaller workable pieces so it can be easily passed through a pasta machine.

GRILLED SWORDFISH WITH GRILLED ARTICHOKES AND A DRIED TOMATO AND ROCKET SALAD

SEARED TUNA WITH HERBS AND LEEKS AND FRESH HORSERADISH AND OLIVE OIL DRESSING

Serves 6 as a main course

250g fresh horseradish, peeled and finely grated
extra virgin olive oil
salt and pepper
3 cups Savoy cabbage, finely julienned
6 tablespoons red wine vinegar
6 tuna steaks, 2 cm thick
$^{1}/_{2}$ cup mixed chopped herbs: thyme, sage, rosemary, basil, parsley
3 large leeks, cleaned, blanched whole and cut into 6 cm pieces

Mix the freshly grated horseradish with some extra virgin olive oil and season to taste with salt only. Dress the cabbage with some extra virgin olive oil and the red wine vinegar. Cover the tuna pieces with the herbs, heat some olive oil in a pan and sear the herbed tuna for 1 minute on each side. Season to taste. Rest in a warm spot for 15 minutes. Arrange the cabbage and pieces of leek on plates, slice the tuna as you would rare meat and lay on the leek. Dress with the horseradish.

OSSO BUCO

Serves 6 as a main course

6 pieces osso buco (veal shank from the hind leg, cut across the bone), about 5 cm thick
1 cup plain flour
olive oil
4 medium onions, peeled and cut into 2 cm chunks
salt and pepper
6 ripe Roma tomatoes, puréed
dry white wine
1 tablespoon plain flour, extra
2 cups fresh borlotti beans, shelled (optional)
1 cup flat-leaf parsley, roughly chopped
5 cloves garlic, crushed

Dust the osso buco with the plain flour, heat some olive oil in a skillet and brown the meat lightly. In a pot large enough to hold all the osso buco, sauté the onions in a little olive oil until they are transparent but not coloured. Arrange the osso buco on top of the onions, season a little with salt and pepper and add the tomatoes and wine so that the meat is just covered. Bring to the boil, lower the heat and simmer, covered, for 90 minutes. Turn the osso buco, remove half a cup of the liquid and mix with extra plain flour. Return this mixture to the pot, add the borlotti beans, parsley and garlic, and simmer for another 30-45 minutes. Season to taste and serve.

GRILLED SWORDFISH WITH GRILLED ARTICHOKES AND A DRIED TOMATO AND ROCKET SALAD

Serves 6 as a main course

6 pieces swordfish, about 1 cm thick
extra virgin olive oil
young rocket leaves
6 char-grilled artichokes
$^{1}/_{2}$ cup dried tomato dressing (see recipe this page)

Coat the swordfish in a little extra virgin olive oil and grill. Serve with the rocket leaves and char-grilled artichokes. Dress with the dried tomato dressing.

DRIED TOMATO DRESSING

Makes about 2 cups

8 dried tomatoes, cut into small dice
1 celery heart, cut into small dice
1 roast red capsicum, skinned and diced
1 roast yellow capsicum, skinned and diced
flesh of 1 tomato, seeded and diced
$^{1}/_{2}$ medium red onion, diced
2 tablespoons Aeolian capers
4 tablespoons extra virgin olive oil
salt and pepper

Mix all of the ingredients together in a bowl. Season to taste and allow to marinate for about 30 minutes.

PIGEON AND BLACK FIG SALAD

Serves 4 as a main course

4 pigeons, trimmed at the wings and neck
extra virgin olive oil
salt and pepper
80g young, first-cut rocket leaves
6 ripe, soft black figs (the Black Genoa variety
are good), cut into quarters
balsamic vinegar

Preheat the oven to 240°C. Place the pigeons in a
baking dish, rub with olive oil and season with
pepper. Roast for 10–12 minutes, keeping the
pigeons quite pink. Remove from the oven and
rest for a further 10 minutes. Take the breasts off
the bone and remove the legs. Make a salad with
the rocket, figs, olive oil and balsamic vinegar.
Season to taste, toss with the pigeon breasts and
legs, then serve.

GRILLED RED EMPEROR PIECES TOSSED IN FRESH HERBS WITH A RAGU OF ZUCCHINI, PEARL ONIONS AND CAPSICUM

Serves 6 as a main course

18 pieces zucchini, cut into 5 cm lengths
9 pearl onions, cut in half lengthways
18 pieces of yellow and red capsicum, about
3 cm x 5 cm
$1/4$ cup extra virgin olive oil, with 4 cloves garlic
minced into it
salt and pepper
18 pieces red emperor (or other reef fish), each
about 50g each
1 cup finely chopped mixed herbs: parsley, sage,
thyme, oregano, rosemary
extra virgin olive oil, extra

Place the vegetables in a large bowl and toss with
the olive oil and season to taste. Grill them on a
flat grill or a barbecue, turning the vegetables
constantly with an egg slice for 5–7 minutes until
they are golden and beginning to char but still a
little firm. Toss the red emperor pieces with the
herbs, season with salt and pepper, pour over a
little extra virgin olive oil and grill, turning on
each side until the fish is done. Serve the fish on
top of the grilled vegetables. (The vegetables will
taste better if they cool a little after grilling.)

ROAST BLACK ANGUS SIRLOIN WITH FARRO AND ROAST CELERIAC IN RED WINE SAUCE

Serves 6 as a main course

Farro (*Triticum dicocum*) is thought to be the
ancestor of modern wheat. Italy grows and exports
excellent farro. It is usually available at good
specialist produce stores, is easy to use and makes a
deliciously useful accompaniment to meat, fish or
vegetables. Farro also adds to a hearty soup in much
the same way as barley.

1 small onion, diced
1 small carrot, diced
1 celery heart, diced
2 cloves garlic, minced
extra virgin olive oil
200g farro (pearl barley may be substituted)
2 ripe Roma tomatoes, peeled and chopped
1 litre veal stock, not reduced (see recipe page 39)
salt and pepper
$1/2$ cup chopped flat-leaf parsley
1–1.2 kg piece Black Angus sirloin, heavily marbled,
trimmed
2 bulbs celeriac, peeled and cut into 12 wedges
300 ml red wine reduction (see recipe page 39)

Lightly fry the onion, carrot, celery and garlic in
2 tablespoons of olive oil for 1 minute until soft.
Add the farro, tomatoes and veal stock. Simmer until
the farro is cooked but still 'al dente'. Season to
taste and add the chopped parsley. Rub the sirloin
with olive oil, season with freshly cracked pepper
and roast in a pre-heated 220°C oven for about
10–12 minutes. Remove from the oven and rest the
meat for at least 20 minutes. Blanch the celeriac
wedges in boiling salted water until they have
softened a little, about 5 minutes. Drain well, toss
with a little olive oil so they are coated, season with
salt and pepper and bake in the oven for 10 minutes
until golden. To serve, slice the sirloin and arrange
on a plate with the farro and celeriac wedges and a
little of the hot red wine sauce to finish.

TOASTED PANETTONE WITH CHERRIES AND MASCARPONE

RUBY GRAPEFRUIT JELLY WITH VANILLA GELATO

Serves 10

For the vanilla gelato
200g caster sugar
8 egg yolks
1 litre fresh cream
2 vanilla beans, seeds scraped

Beat the sugar and egg yolks together until they are pale. Heat the cream until it almost boils. Add the vanilla seeds and whisk in the sugar and egg mixture. Place on a low heat and stir continuously with a wooden spoon until the mixture thickens and coats the back of a spoon. Cool completely before churning. Once churned, spoon into trays and freeze.

For the grapefruit salad
200g cumquats, macerated overnight in 200g sugar
2 fresh bay leaves, julienned
10 fresh peppercorns
4 ruby grapefruit, segmented
4 yellow grapefruit, segmented

Heat a saucepan on the stove on high for 2 minutes or until really hot. Add the macerated cumquats with their sugar and cook until the sugar reaches the soft ball stage. Remove from the heat and add the bay leaves and peppercorns. Cool completely. Add the grapefruit segments.

For the jelly
1 litre ruby grapefruit juice
130g caster sugar
14 gelatine leaves, soaked

Add the strained grapefruit juice to a saucepan and warm. Add the sugar and soaked gelatine leaves. Stir thoroughly but do not whisk. Skim any excess scum from the top, then pour into individual moulds to set. Cut the gelato into a desired shape and place on a plate. Demould the jelly onto the gelato. Scatter the grapefruit salad around the gelato.

TOASTED PANETTONE WITH CHERRIES AND MASCARPONE

Serves 4 as a Christmas dessert

500g cherries, pitted
375 ml sweet wine
8 small slices Italian panettone, about 1 cm thick
8 tablespoons fresh mascarpone
icing sugar

In a bowl, cover the cherries with the sweet wine and allow to macerate for at least 2 hours. Toast the panettone pieces then arrange half of the cherries on 4 of the pieces. Spread 1 spoonful of mascarpone over each. Top each with another piece of panettone, then the remaining cherries. Spread 1 spoonful of mascarpone over each and dust with icing sugar.

STONE FRUITS WITH CRACKED PEPPER AND PISTACHIO TUILLE

Serves 10

For the tuille
240g egg whites
350g caster sugar
200g melted butter
300g plain flour
150g cracked pepper
250g pistachios, chopped

Whisk the egg whites and sugar until it reaches a stiff meringue consistency. Slowly add the melted butter, whisking continuously. Fold in the flour by hand. Refrigerate until needed. Spread the mixture into circles. Sprinkle with cracked pepper and chopped pistachios. Bake in a 180°C oven for 5–8 minutes or until just cooked (light brown). Mould the tuilles over a rolling pin while still hot.

For the stone fruits
5 nectarines
5 apricots
5 plums
5 peaches
80g brown sugar
50g unsalted butter

Slice the fruits in half and deseed. Arrange on a baking tray with the seeded side up. Sprinkle generously with brown sugar and dot each fruit with a small cube of butter. Bake in a 180°C oven for 10 minutes or until just soft but not disintegrated. Remove the fruits from any liquid and cool. Place half of each of the 4 fruits onto each plate. Serve with tuilles.

ESPRESSO ICE-CREAM TERRINE

Serves 6–8

For the espresso gelato
200g caster sugar
8 egg yolks
1 litre pouring cream
1 tablespoon ground coffee
6 espresso coffees

Beat together the sugar and egg yolks until pale. Heat the cream and the ground coffee until it almost boils. Whisk in the sugar and egg mixture. Cook over a lot heat, stirring continuously with a wooden spoon until the mixture thickens and coats the back of a spoon. Add the espresso coffees. Cool before churning.

For the chocolate gelato
200g caster sugar
8 egg yolks
1 litre pouring cream
200g dark chocolate buds
150 ml dark cocoa liqueur

Beat together the sugar and egg yolks until pale. Heat the cream until it almost boils. Whisk in the sugar and egg mixture. Cook over a low heat, stirring continuously with a wooden spoon until the mixture thickens and coats the back of a spoon. Pour the hot mixture over the chocolate buds and stir until the chocolate melts. Add the liqueur. Cool before churning.

For the hazelnut gelato
200g caster sugar
8 egg yolks
1 litre pouring cream
1 tablespoon hazelnut paste
180g roasted hazelnuts, ground

Beat together the sugar and egg yolks until pale. Heat the cream until it almost boils. Whisk in the sugar and egg mixture. Cook over a low heat, stirring continuously with a wooden spoon until the mixture thickens and coats the back of a spoon. Add the hazelnut paste and mix well. Cool. Add the ground roasted hazelnuts. Churn.

To assemble
Spoon the chocolate gelato into a terrine mould to fill one third. Freeze for 2 hours. Repeat the same process with the hazelnut gelato and the espresso gelato. Freeze overnight. To serve, unmould by enclosing the mould in a warm towel. Turn out the terrine onto a tray to serve. Always use a hot knife to cut.

WHERE THERE'S LIGHT, THERE'S SHADE. CHIAROSCURO.

3

LIGHT

...A WARM, AMBER GLOW...

Peter Langan was one of the most successful restaurateurs in the London of the 1960s and '70s. His restaurants, Odins, the first, then later Langan's Bistro and Langan's Brasserie caught the mood of the times and were packed with *tout Londres*; rock stars, villains and cabinet ministers jostled for entrée. Actor Michael Caine was a partner in two of his ventures. When asked for his philosophy on restaurant creation, he would say, 'The most important thing in a restaurant is lighting. If the girl opposite you looks like the most beautiful girl in the world, and the food's all right, you'll come back time and again. If the lighting's bad, no matter how good the food is, you won't enjoy it.'

Langan would send trucks to Paris with orders to comb the flea markets for old cafe wall lights with parchment shades. The light shone through the old parchment with a warm, amber glow, as close to candlelight as you could get without using candles and with more illumination.

But that was then. And *bel mondo* is now and is, according to architect Luigi Rosselli, 'a very, very complex building to light':

'We started with coloured drawings, just to imagine how it was to be. The general concept, because it was such a large space, was to work on the contrast between the small scale and the large scale, the theatrical and the intimate. These were the words in the brief from the clients, they wanted it theatrical and romantic.

'So the large scale is the high ceilinged building, and the small scale is the table environment, the waiters' stations and the bar, with an intermediate scale being the raised kitchen. These are the three arenas for lighting.

'For the small scale we needed warm, glowing light for people to look their best, and that was achieved with table lights, which we designed. They had to be battery driven because of the heritage restriction of not being able to cut through the floors. The table lamp is ideal, because you get a light which comes from below, shining upward, which is more flattering than a light from above, shining down.

'Then for the larger space, we wanted to contrast with cool lighting, a very deep blue for the cathedral ceiling, which was difficult to achieve, again with the heritage limitations. In my mind it still could be better.

'So there is the overall theatrical element: the soft glow from the tables; the blue light of the ceiling; a glowing light from the bar; and the fireworks in the kitchen which is also lit by down lights, not fluorescents, in keeping with the general plan.'

BEL MONDO MOMENTS

THE HEART ATTACK

We'd been open only three months. It was a very busy lunch and all had gone well. One of our newer regulars had just finished and was waiting for the elevator to take him down the building and back to the office when suddenly he collapsed. Our maître d' took charge, phoned security and paramedics, then made the gentleman comfortable, making sure he was still breathing. In no time he was taken off to hospital. Ten days later he was back having lunch at *bel mondo* and very thankful to our maître d'.

"THE INVENTION OF COOKING MAY WELL HAVE BEEN THE DECISIVE FACTOR THAT ENABLED MAN TO SHIFT FROM AN ESSENTIALLY ANIMAL EXISTENCE TO A TRULY HUMAN ONE."

JEAN-MARIE BOURRE

Where there's light, there's shade. Chiaroscuro. 'Kee-aro-skooro', light and shade. The cloud that passes over the kitchen when things go wrong. The bickering that picks away at the edges when people don't – well, don't agree, don't get on, don't see the same way, aren't in the same movie. If a patron senses such discord, a yelling and a crashing from the kitchen, surly, preoccupied service, it's dangerous for the long term health of the business.

A restaurant – even the largest – is a small business with a hot room full of overstressed people wielding sharp knives at its heart. There are not many businesses where 200 customers walk in every night not knowing what they want, make up their mind on the spot from a list of options, which you then have to supply exactly as they demand, turning the words describing their order on the page into a reality on a plate that meets – or exceeds – their expectations.

It is a business that requires people of different temperaments – cooks, waiters, managers, accountants – to work together to secure a result. It operates on the smallest of profit margins, on a knife edge between success and failure, pushed and pulled and buffeted by fashion, form, the economy (in lean times, the first thing people give up is eating out at the top end) and blind luck. It is, quite simply, a recipe for disaster, and you wonder why sane people insist on doing it.

But they do. Every month, Restaurant and Catering, the industry body, receives around 50 applications for membership: that's around 600 new restaurants a year. For those who insist on following this insane course (remember, most new restaurants close within the first year of their operation) it is very important to have your eyes wide open. It's no use saying, as you prepare to open the doors, that it'll be all right on the night, because chances are it won't. Get it right before you light the stoves.

It's a fairly safe bet that people won't beat a path to every new restaurant's door. They're not waiting with tongues hanging out for your food and, besides, even if what you have to offer is sensational, so is the offer down the road. Whatever city you live in, take a stroll downtown and do an audit on the number of restaurants, cafes and eating establishments per block. And you will notice they open and close like a butterfly's wings. The failure rate is so high that even the Manfredi family, with a 13 year track record, thought long and hard before serving their first customer. And there was one added complication.

QUANDO L'ACQUA BOLLE BUTTA SUBITO I MACCHERONI.

WHEN THE WATER BOILS, THROW IN THE MACARONI (A COOK'S WAY OF SAYING SEIZE THE DAY).

(FROM THE ITALIAN KITCHEN)

Between leaving the old restaurant and starting the new one, Julie and Stefano's marriage broke up. They were to have been partners in the restaurant. At that stage, Franca, Stefano's mother, was a third partner, and there was a fourth 'silent partner'.

'The breakup of our marriage meant that we had a financial partner pull out because he felt uncomfortable about that. He wanted us to stay together but in fact, that would have been worse, it would have been much more volatile. Now, every time he comes into the restaurant he makes a point of telling us he's kicking himself.

"GOOD FOOD, GOOD EATING, IS ABOUT BLOOD AND ORGANS, CRUELTY AND DECAY."
ANTHONY BOURDAIN

'But his departure laid the ground for Franck Crouvezier to come in as a partner. And that has worked out for the best. We're much happier, because silent partners rarely work out; they are never silent, and never partners. They have nothing to put into the business except money, and money is probably the least important of the ingredients required for success.

'At the beginning, we had to have a meeting to set up contracts between all the partners and we all needed, by law, to have individual counsel. It came to a head one afternoon in Julie's lawyer's office, where all four of us had our lawyers present, and they were all shaking their heads and saying that, because of the marriage breakup, this is dangerous, and goes completely against what we would advise each of you.

'At that point, I said nobody is leaving here until we nut out an in-principle agreement that says we can proceed because that is what we want to do. All of us individually know we want this, we know we all have different things to bring to the partnership and the company, and we know this is going to be a very successful restaurant.' ■

STEFANO MANFREDI

Julie Manfredi-Hughes was at the other end of this personal and professional dilemma.

'I found myself dealing with the emotional side of losing Steve as a husband and, at the same time, a whole new set of developments in my professional life. I'd gone back to university and I was doing post graduate business studies, so I was also implementing new strategies into our business life so we could move from Ultimo to a site that would sustain us through the next five or ten years.

'I guess I treated it like anybody would treat a personal crisis. I had to learn to put boundaries around the personal crisis and go to work. We never talked about how we would work together. We just did.

'There was the personal way of finding the strength to carry on, and then there was what I'd call the structural and political arena. I've never been a raging feminist, but I've grown up with the generation who've had to deal with the revolution that has taken place with women's role in society and in the way we hold property, and our financial independence. I found myself running headlong into these issues.

'An anecdote that best describes this is one where I remember sitting across the table from our company solicitor, who was very supportive of both of us through all of this, and was concerned for the business decisions we were making. He said to me, "why don't you just go off and find your own life? How can you possibly stay in this situation?" I said to him – this is my life. And just because I'm losing my husband, I don't want it to also mean I'm losing my business, and the next stage, which is my career.

'That was the driving force for me. Not ideal, not as I would have wanted it to be, but nonetheless, the way it was. And working creatively within the constraints. That's what it has been for me.' ■

JULIE MANFREDI-HUGHES

"WITHOUT LIPIDS, AND THEREFORE WITHOUT FAT, OUR NOURISHMENT WOULD BE A SAD AND INEFFICIENT AFFAIR – MORTAL IN EVERY SENSE OF THE WORD."

JEAN-MARIE BOURRE

Light is also a word that has, in recent times, been attached to food, although such a usage is not to everyone's taste. Writing in *The Spectator*, Imperative Cooking columnist Digby Anderson fulminates against it: 'By "light" is, of course, meant tasteless, weak, insipid, low in energy, highly filtered, flimsy and fluffy. Indeed, light is rather a useful concept. It gathers together all the different ways in which food and drink can be awful.'

Its use does tend to underscore the way in which food, for many, has become a battleground, a problem rather than a pleasure, each meal choice needing to be analysed to ascertain which of its components are 'good', and which 'bad'. At various times in the recent past, red meat, cheese, celery and soy beans have all been fingered as 'bad foods'. Discussing this phenomenon at some length, journalist Richard Girling concluded 'you don't have to be a scientist to believe all the stuff written about food. You have to be an idiot.'

We have a very simple philosophy. We use fresh ingredients, we use them at their peak, we cook them in a relatively simple way and we present them in a very unassuming and non-threatening way. This is the Italian style. We do use oil to cook, which is to say we use fat, but fat is an essential part of the diet.

But there is a lighter side to food. Food can be witty, silly, ironic – or just plain fun. From time to time we create 'theme' dinners.

Another way of eating lightly is the snack. Snack, in Italian, is spuntino, from a curious verb, *spuntare*, with a variety of meanings from 'to sprout' to 'to appear suddenly'. In the theatre you find the word *spunto*, or cue. So spuntini (plural of *spuntino*) could be seen as cues to the meal to come that appear suddenly, sprouting on the bar. It could also have some link with the idea of spontaneity.

Mainly bar food, spuntini are the Italian equivalent of the Spanish tapas, the Middle eastern and Greek mezes, the French canapés (although, strictly speaking, canapés are only little sandwiches) or *amuse-gueule*, literally 'amuse-mouth'. Spuntini from the Antibar might include:

Steamed asparagus with a garlic maionese
Roast salmon with salmon eggs rolled in poppy seed
Marinated artichoke filled with hot smoked river trout
Grilled cuttlefish with eggplant and a salsa piccante
Prawn and tomato on sourdough crostini
Smoked salmon, lamb's lettuce and celeriac salad
Roast golf ball chilli with anchovy and roast garlic
Rare roast beef fillet and green olive roll
Tuna carpaccio roll Mediterranean style
Pizzette
Deep-fried zucchini flowers stuffed with gruyère
Chicken rotolini
Tuna and swordfish carpaccio rolls with Sicilian caper salsa
Roast polenta, pecorino and prosciutto
Crostini with olive paste and goat's cheese, capsicum, eggplant and pesto, chicken livers and onions, smoked salmon

MARINETTI'S FUTURISM

Futurism was an influential art movement with political implications founded by the Italian poet Filippo Tommaso Marinetti (known universally as Marinetti) at the beginning of the century. Its aim was to blast away the past and embrace the future, an idealised future where speed, the machine and technology would free man from slavery. Its first manifesto was published in 1909. In 1930, Marinetti published 'The Manifesto of Futurist Cooking' in the *Gazzetta del Popolo* in Turin, which was followed in 1932 by *The Futurist Cookbook*, co-written with the painter Luigi Colombo Fillia. In the foreword of the 1989 edition, British culinary academic Lesley Chamberlain calls this book a 'unique joke' and writes of it that it is '... funny, almost slapstick in its

attacks on bourgeois habits, stuffy professors and the war between the sexes'.

Marinetti wrote: 'This futurist cooking of ours, tuned to high speeds like the motor of an aeroplane, will seem to some traditionalists both mad and dangerous.'

But most infuriating to the Italians of the day, who failed to see the joke, he wrote: 'we believe necessary ... [the] abolition of pastasciutta (dried pasta), an absurd Italian gastronomic religion', which he pronounced, promoted '... lassitude, pessimism, nostalgic inactivity and neutralism.'

The food itself is more poetry than reality, and includes such dishes as Sausages Floating in Beer, Dusted with Crystallized Pistachios; Marinated Eel Stuffed with Frozen Milanese Minestrone and Dates which Themselves have been Stuffed with Anchovies. You get the picture.

Those who came to the Futurist Dinner at the *Restaurant Manfredi* still talk about it. It comprised Intuitive Salad; Edible Landscape, Preserved Fish + Chocolate = Professor; Sculpted Meat (a version of which is in

The Futurist Cookbook); and finished with Breasts Get the Point. The food was enjoyed in spite of being punctuated by the random sounds of aircraft taking off, grinding metal, steam train whistles and racing engines that accompanied it.

For us in the kitchen it was exhilarating to create and then produce a meal that was part fantasy, part history but which still managed to taste wonderful. It is important to remember, for the New World, which has only recently taken up gastronomy, that we need not be serious all the time. And it is no accident that it was an Italian who chose to publish a tongue in cheek political manifesto in the form of a poetic cookbook.

Preserved Fish + Chocolate = Professor

"THIS IS ULTIMATELY WHAT WE DO. WE HAVE THIS CREATURE WE'VE BUILT TO PLEASE PEOPLE."
STEFANO MANFREDI

'I recently came across a meat product that could only be described as light, but also delicious. One of the most interesting aspects of the 1999 Royal Easter Show was the Alternative Farming pavilion. It is here that many wild and wacky, as well as ingenious, schemes from rural Australia are given their first public airing. Among the jams and preserves, the goanna oil, the emu eggs and unusual fashion accessories made with emu hide, enthusiastic exhibitors were discussing the virtues of hemp as a source of fibre for clothing.

'My interest was directed toward a pair of Boer goats – a doe and a buck, seeming to like the constant attention of the crowd. As the name suggests, this breed is from South Africa, having been selectively bred over 50 or more years specifically for their meat. Consequently, the Boer is considered far superior to any

other goat for meat production because of its rapid weight gain, heavy muscling and high fertility. Typically, these goats tend to give birth to twins and they can manage this three times every two years.

'The exporting of genetics began in January 1987 when embryos were taken from female Boer goats in Zimbabwe by Landcorp Farming NZ, and implanted into local New Zealand goats on Soames Island, the country's maximum quarantine facility, in May the same year. This herd formed the basis of the international breeding stock that was consequently sent to Canada, the USA, Indonesia, England, India, France, Malaysia and Denmark. An Australian group did the same in 1988, breeding the goats at the Terraweena quarantine facility until they were released in November 1995 to form the basis of Australia's herd.

'Earlier this year, I was sent a Boer goat carcass by George Macdonald to "cook up" and evaluate. It cooks in a very similar way to the Illabo suckling lamb in terms of cooking times for a leg. It has a beautiful sweet and delicate flavour, but because it's very lean it needs care. It can be cooked as we are doing it at the moment – roasting a leg at 260°C for twenty minutes, and

resting for about 30 minutes. It is not as fatty as Illabo lamb, so you have to be careful not to cook it for a long long time unless you cook it very slowly. A good way is to crust a leg with salt and roast it over two or three hours at 120–150°C. It's a meat that also takes on the flavour of its accompaniments, for example, the traditional braising herbs, thyme and rosemary, and it is particularly good with mushrooms or larded with garlic.

'George's company, Intercapital, has formed a joint venture with farmers David and Sally Rogers to raise Boer goats for meat on their property Elms Hall, Vacy, north of Maitland, in New South Wales. David Rogers is enthusiastic about the results so far; not only have the Boers improved the quality of the herd, but he can graze ten goats on an area of land usually reserved for one cow. Given their high fertility rates and fast growing properties, there is real potential for a reasonably good return. There have been Boer goat farmers in Texas reporting a threefold increase in returns over cattle farming.' ■

STEFANO MANFREDI

But let's snuff the chapter on light with a quotation from a Neapolitan writer, the most satisfying we have found yet on coffee, that incomparably light beverage, which provides the perfect finale to any meal. Its quality can enhance or degrade the meal it follows, and its preparation has been perfected by the Italians.

Coffee, Luciano de Crescenzo writes, is: 'not simply a liquid, but something that is, so to speak, halfway between liquid and air; a concoction that, as soon as it touches the palate, is sublimated and instead of going down goes up and up until it enters the brain where it nestles in a companionable sort of a way so that for hours on end a man can be working and thinking, "what a wonderful cup of coffee I had this morning".'

RECIPES

RECIPES

BEAN, ASPARAGUS AND FRIED PROSCIUTTO SALAD

Serves 6 as a first course

200g green beans, stems removed
500g asparagus
1 clove garlic, minced
extra virgin olive oil
handful parsley, chopped
6 slices prosciutto

Cook the beans and asparagus in plenty of boiling salted water until 'al dente'. Drain and dress immediately with the olive oil, garlic and chopped parsley. Fry the prosciutto in a small amount of olive oil until crisp. When it has cooled enough, crumble it over the beans and asparagus as a final dressing, then serve.

SPAGHETTINI WITH TASMANIAN SALMON ROE AND CHIVES

Serves 6 as a first course

200g spaghettini (see recipe this page)
6 tablespoons extra virgin olive oil
1 bunch chives, chopped
salt
200g Tasmanian salmon roe

Cook the pasta in plenty of boiling salted water so that it is still quite 'al dente'. The pasta needs to be very textured for this dish so it's imperative that the pasta is a little undercooked. Once it is ready, refresh it immediately in cold running water until it has cooled. Do not leave it soaking in water for a prolonged period as it will get soggy. Drain it well, toss with the olive oil and the chives, seasoning to taste. Distribute the dressed pasta on serving plates and dollop a spoonful of roe on each. This dish is served at room temperature without parmesan.

For the spaghettini

Make a well in about 100g plain flour. Add enough whole eggs (it should take 1 or 2) so that when they are worked into the flour, the dough is not sticky and not dry. Compensate by adding more flour if too sticky, or more egg if too dry. Cut the pasta dough into smaller workable pieces so it can be easily passed through a pasta machine. Roll it until the pasta is smooth and silky. Pass the sheets through the spaghettini cutter and hang to dry a little. Cook the pasta in an abundant amount of rapidly boiling, salted water until 'al dente'. Drain the pasta and dress with some olive oil so that the strands don't stick to one another as they cool.

PAN-FRIED VEAL TENDERLOIN WITH ROAST EGGPLANT, PEPERONATA AND BOCCONCINI

Serves 4 as a first course

For the eggplant
salt
1–2 medium-sized eggplants, cut into
1 cm thick slices
olive oil

Sprinkle a little salt on both sides of the eggplant slices. Leave for 10 minutes, then pat each slice dry with a towel. Brush each slice with olive oil, place on a baking tray and roast in a 220°C oven until the eggplant is golden brown. Remove from the oven and allow to cool.

For the peperonata
6 tablespoons extra virgin olive oil
2 large red capsicums, cut into large pieces
2 medium onions, cut into chunks
2 cloves garlic, minced
4 egg tomatoes, roughly chopped
handful basil
salt and pepper

Heat the olive oil in a large saucepan, then add the capsicums, onions and garlic. Turn up the heat and stir with a wooden spoon for a couple of minutes until the contents wilt a little. Add the tomatoes and simmer for 20 minutes, stirring occasionally. Add the basil, season to taste and allow to cool.

To assemble
extra virgin olive oil
4 slices veal tenderloin, cut 5 mm thick,
then each slice halved
salt and pepper
4 bocconcini, thinly sliced

Heat some olive oil in a pan and sear the veal briefly on each side. Season to taste and then rest for at least 10 minutes. Place an eggplant slice on each plate and spoon over some of the peperonata. Place a piece of veal on top then add some slices of bocconcini. Add another eggplant slice, some more peperonata, veal, bocconcini and finally a slice of eggplant. You should have a stack like a double-decker sandwich.

CARPACCIO OF SILVER PERCH WITH CELERIAC AND LAMB'S LETTUCE

Serves 4 as a first course

1 silver perch fillet, boned and thinly sliced
extra virgin olive oil
salt and pepper
1 medium-sized celeriac bulb, peeled and cut into julienne
2 cups clean lamb's lettuce
juice of $1/2$ lemon

Lay the slices of silver perch on each serving plate. Sprinkle with extra virgin olive oil and season to taste. Toss the celeriac julienne and the lamb's tongue lettuce together in a bowl with some olive oil and lemon juice. Season to taste. Serve the salad with the perch carpaccio.

SPAGHETTINI WITH TASMANIAN SALMON ROE AND CHIVES

HARBOUR PRAWN AND BASIL FRITTATA

Makes 1 single serve

olive oil
2 eggs
1 tablespoon grated parmesan
salt and pepper
10–12 harbour prawns, cooked and peeled
1 handful rocket leaves, thinly sliced
1 tablespoon pesto (see recipe page 33)

Heat a little olive oil in a skillet until it is just smoking. Beat the eggs lightly with the parmesan, season to taste and pour into the hot pan. The frittata should be quite wide and spread over the pan quite thinly. It should take only a couple of minutes to cook. Distribute the prawns so that they heat on the frittata. Transfer to a plate, pile the rocket leaves in the middle of the frittata and drizzle the pesto on.

STRACCI WITH SAFFRON, SAVOY CABBAGE AND BROAD BEANS

Serves 8–10 as a first course

$1/2$ cup thinly shaved parmesan pieces
500 ml milk
$1/2$ Savoy cabbage, trimmed of the tough outside leaves
saffron threads
basic pasta dough (see recipe this page)
salt and pepper
1 $1/2$ cups double peeled broad beans, blanched quickly

Soak the parmesan pieces in the milk for 1 hour. Steam the cabbage in a little water until the leaves have softened. Work the saffron threads into the pasta dough then roll out the dough into thin sheets. Cut the sheets into large rectangles about 6–7 cm square. Place the milk and parmesan in a bain marie, or a bowl set over a pot of boiling water and stir until they become totally incorporated and velvety. Season the sauce. Cook the pasta sheets until 'al dente' and place them on each plate. Cut the cabbage leaves about the same shape and size as the pasta and place them on top. Scatter the broad beans over and finish by dressing with the parmesan sauce. Serve hot.

For the pasta dough

Make a well in about 100g plain flour. Add enough whole eggs (it should take 1 or 2) so that when they are worked into the flour, the dough is not sticky and not dry. Compensate by adding more flour if too sticky, or more egg if too dry.

HARBOUR PRAWN AND BASIL FRITTATA

BARBECUED SUCKLING LAMB CUTLETS 'AL DRAGONCELLO'

MUD CRAB WITH POLENTA, TOMATO AND CHILLI SAUCE

Serves 4 as a main course

2 live mud crabs, each 700–800g
soft polenta (see recipe this page)
tomato and chilli sauce (see recipe this page)
freshly grated parmesan
fresh chilli, seeded and chopped (optional)
olive oil, extra

Drop the crabs in very salty boiling water (150g rock salt for every litre of water) for 12 minutes then leave to cool, away from the heat, in the cooking water for 10 minutes before draining. Take the four large claws from the bodies and crack them using a kitchen mallet, leaving them mostly intact but allowing access to the meat. Remove the meat from the rest of the crab and set aside. Place the soft polenta on a serving plate. Sprinkle a little parmesan on top, then add some of the tomato and chilli sauce and finally the cooked mud crab on the very top. The cracked claws accompany the polenta on the top or on the side. The polenta should be served immediately, spooned from the serving plate. Extra chilli can be served in a little olive oil on the side.

SOFT POLENTA

1.5 litres water
salt
250g coarse polenta

Bring the salted water to the boil then slowly add the polenta, stirring constantly with a wooden spoon or whisk until the polenta comes away from the sides of the saucepan. Reduce the heat to a simmer and place a lid on. Simmer for about 20 minutes, giving the polenta a good stir every 5 minutes. The polenta should be soft and tender, ready for serving.

TOMATO AND CHILLI SAUCE

2 leeks, cleaned and cut into rounds
2 chillies, seeded and chopped
2 cloves garlic, minced
extra virgin olive oil
2 kg ripe tomatoes, peeled and chopped
basil leaves
salt and pepper

Fry the leeks, chillies and garlic in olive oil until they have softened. Add the tomatoes and simmer for 10–15 minutes. Add the basil and season to taste.

DUCK STOCK

Makes 2 litres

3 duck carcasses
2 onions, peeled and halved
1 leek, cleaned and cut into large rounds
1 carrot, peeled and cut into large rounds
1 celery heart
4 cloves garlic, peeled and left whole

Lightly roast the duck carcasses for 20 minutes in a preheated 180°C oven. Place the duck carcasses and all the remaining ingredients into a large stock pot and cover with fresh water. Simmer for 3 hours, skimming off any impurities that rise to the top. Strain and refridgerate until the fat solidifies on the surface. Remove the fat. Reheat the stock and reduce to 2 litres.

BARBECUED SUCKLING LAMB CUTLETS 'AL DRAGONCELLO'

Serves 4 as a main course

24 lamb cutlets from the best end of the rack, trimmed
3 tablespoons extra virgin olive oil
salt and pepper
1 cup Savoy cabbage, finely sliced
1 tablespoon balsamic vinegar
$1/4$ cup salsa dragoncello (see recipe this page)

Place the cutlets on a plate, brush lightly with some of the olive oil and barbecue for 2–3 minutes on each side. Meanwhile, season to taste and dress the cabbage with the remaining olive oil and balsamic vinegar and arrange it on plates. Arrange the cutlets on top of the cabbage. Season to taste and serve with the salsa dragoncello as an accompaniment.

SALSA DRAGONCELLO

Makes 1 cup of salsa

3 slices day old bread, crusts removed
3 tablespoons red wine vinegar
$1/2$ cup fresh tarragon leaves, taken off the stem
1 clove garlic, minced
$1/4$ cup extra virgin olive oil
salt and pepper

Moisten the bread with the vinegar until it is completely absorbed. Place the bread, the tarragon and the garlic into a food processor and turn it on, pouring the olive oil in slowly until it is well blended. Season to taste and store in a jar in the refrigerator until needed. It will last quite a long time.

ROAST DUCK 'AL MAZZANO' WITH CORZETTI AND A PUREE OF CELERIAC AND GARLIC

Serves 6 as a main course

For the purée

500g celeriac, peeled and cut into quarters
50g butter
salt and pepper
1 whole bulb garlic, roasted

Simmer the celeriac in water only until the pieces have softened; do not overcook. Drain and place in a food processor with the butter and seasoning, and purée. Check for seasoning and adjust. Roast the garlic until the cloves have lost their firmness but have not turned to a purée. Peel the cloves, cut each into 3 chunks and mix them through the celeriac purée while it is still warm.

For the sauce

180 ml Masi Mazzano Amarone (a rich red wine such as shiraz or a Rhone red can be substituted)
2 cloves garlic, peeled
1 bay leaf
2 onions, peeled and quartered
2 cm length cinnamon quill, left whole
180 ml reduced duck stock (see recipe page 106)
salt and pepper
50g butter

Place the wine, garlic, bay leaf, onions and cinnamon in a saucepan and cook over a medium heat until the liquid has reduced by two-thirds. Add the duck stock and simmer until it has reduced by two-thirds again. Strain out the onion and spices. To serve, season to taste and whisk in the butter at the last moment.

For the corzetti pasta

Make a well in about 100g of plain flour. Add enough whole eggs (it should take 1 or 2) so that when they are worked into the flour, the dough is not sticky and not dry. Compensate by adding more flour if too sticky, or more egg if too dry. Cut the pasta dough into smaller workable pieces so it can be easily passed through a pasta machine. Roll it until the pasta is smooth and silky. Once the dough is made, take small pieces the size of a thumbnail off the large lump. Keeping your fingers well floured, press each piece into the work surface with your thumb so that it is roughly round. This is the form of the corzetti or 'coin'. Cook the corzetti in an abundant amount of rapidly boiling salted water until 'al dente'. Drain them and dress with some olive oil so that they don't stick to one another.

For the duck

6 duck breasts, left on the breastplate
salt

Salt the skin, place the breasts skin side down in a roasting pan and place in a preheated 250°C oven for 8 minutes. This will crisp the skin and remove most of the fat so that the duck pieces are ready for the grill. Place the breasts, skin side down, under the grill for 5–6 minutes to crisp. Take each breast off the bone, slice into 6 pieces, and place these on each plate with some corzetti and sauce. Serve immediately with the purée as accompaniment. This dish is best served with Masi Recioto della Valpolicella Mazzano.

WARM SALAD OF SCHNAPPER, BEANS AND RADICCHIO

Serves 6 as a main course

3 kg schnapper, filleted and boned, skin left on
6 tablespoons extra virgin olive oil
salt and pepper
500g small green beans, cooked in boiling salted water briefly until 'al dente' and allowed to cool
2 radicchio hearts, washed and sliced into thick strips lengthways
6 tablespoons olive oil, extra
2 tablespoons balsamic vinegar

Preheat the oven to 250°C. Cut the fish into 6 roughly even pieces, pulling out any bones with a pair of tweezers. Put the olive oil evenly into two ovenproof skillets and heat until it starts to smoke. Sprinkle some salt on the skin side of each of the schnapper pieces and gently place them, skin side down, in the hot oil. Fry for about 30 seconds, then turn them. Place the skillets in the oven for about 7 minutes, or transfer the fish to a baking dish and bake for 7–10 minutes.

Meanwhile place the beans and radicchio in a large mixing bowl and toss with the extra olive oil and balsamic vinegar, seasoning to taste. Distribute among the 6 serving plates, and place a piece of fish on each. Serve immediately.

PUMPKIN AND TOFFEE PUDDING WITH SPICED TAMARILLO

Serves 10

For the caramel syrup
750 ml sugar
250 ml golden syrup

Boil the sugar and enough water to cover until it reaches about 175°C. Place in the refrigerator until it cools completely. Mix in the golden syrup.

For the tamarillo compote
750 ml dessert wine
750 ml red wine
150g demerara sugar
150g honey
zest and juice of 1 orange
zest and juice of 1 lemon
2–3 vanilla beans, seeds scraped
1 cinnamon quill
1 fresh bay leaf
$1/2$ teaspoon cardamom
12 tamarillos

Place all the ingredients except the tamarillos in a saucepan. Bring to the boil and reduce by half. Strain the mixture. Quickly blanch the tamarillos. Peel and cut in half and add to the reduced liquid. Bring back to the boil, then simmer for 4–5 minutes. Remove from the heat and cool.

For the pudding
200g Queensland Blue pumpkin
250g unsalted butter
375g caster sugar
1 teaspoon vanilla essence
4 eggs
500g plain flour
$2 1/2$ teaspoons baking powder
pinch salt
180 ml milk

Cut the pumpkin into large pieces, leaving the skin on. Place in a steamer and steam until very well cooked. Carefully remove the pumpkin while still hot and scoop out the flesh with a spoon. Place the flesh in clean muslin cloth layers and squeeze out all of the moisture.

Cream together the butter and sugar until quite pale. Add the vanilla essence and 2 whole eggs and 2 egg yolks (reserve the 2 whites). Whisk until clear. Add the sifted flour, baking powder and salt and gently fold into the mixture. Mix in the milk and pumpkin. In another bowl, whisk the reserved egg whites until stiff. Fold into the pumpkin mixture. Fill small buttered and sugared moulds three-quarters full. Bake in a bain marie or place the moulds in a baking pan with water coming halfway up the sides and bake at 180°C until cooked through. Turn out of the moulds and place on trays for easy serving. While still hot, pour over the caramel and golden syrup sauce so the puddings absorb the syrup and become moist. Warm the pumpkin puddings in the microwave for $1 1/2$ minutes. Place in the middle of the plates and spoon the compote around, then drizzle syrup around the compote.

POACHED PEACHES WITH ZABAGLIONE

Serves 6

6 medium-sized freestone peaches
6 tablespoons sugar
750 ml sweet wine
4 egg yolks
3 tablespoons caster sugar
4 tablespoons hazelnut liqueur

Place the peaches, sugar and sweet wine in a saucepan and bring to the boil. Reduce the heat and simmer for 5 minutes. Peel the peaches under cold water, then return to the poaching mixture until needed. Bring some water to the boil in a pot. In a bowl that fits neatly over the pot, place the egg yolks, caster sugar and liqueur and beat with a whisk until the mixture thickens, about 5–6 minutes. Serve the peaches with the zabaglione drizzled over them.

LITTLE CITRUS TARTS WITH LEMONADE FRUIT AND RUBY GRAPEFRUIT SORBETTI

Makes about 30 tarts

For the sweet paste
500g plain flour
200g icing sugar
250g unsalted butter
2 eggs
vanilla essence

In a processor, blend the flour, sugar and butter until the butter coats the flour. Add the eggs and vanilla essence until it all comes together. Shape into a log and rest overnight. Cut a slice from the log and roll out onto a floured surface. Place the pastry into a tartlet shell and trim around the edges. Rest for 2 hours. Bake blind at 140°C until golden (not brown).

For the lemon curd
6 eggs
juice and finely grated zest of 4 lemons
250g caster sugar
200g unsalted butter

For the mandarin curd
6 eggs
6 mandarins (juice of 6, finely grated zest of 4)
250g caster sugar
200g unsalted butter

The method for both the lemon curd and the mandarin curd is identical. In a double saucepan whisk the eggs, juice, zest and sugar until mixture doubles or thickens. Slowly add the butter, being careful not to separate the mixture. Pour into containers to set.

For the lemonade fruit sorbetti
500 ml juice of lemonade fruit
500 ml sugar syrup (made from 250g sugar dissolved in 250 ml water)
1 lemonade fruit, segmented

For the ruby grapefruit sorbetti
500 ml juice of ruby grapefruit
500 ml sugar syrup (made from 250g sugar dissolved in 250 ml water)
1 ruby grapefruit, segmented

The method for both the lemonade fruit sorbetti and the ruby grapefruit sorbetti is identical. Mix the fruit juice with the sugar syrup, add the fruit segments and churn. Freeze until required.

To assemble
Fill some of the tarts with the lemon curd and some with the mandarin curd, scraping the tops so they are perfectly flat. Sprinkle with caster sugar and caramelise with a hot brulée iron or under a very hot grill. Top with scoops of sorbetti.

PASSIONFRUIT, ROCKMELON AND LEMON JELLIES WITH PAPAYA SEMIFREDDO

Serves 10

For the jellies
passionfruit
rockmelon
lemon
champagne
sugar
gelatine leaves

Individually, purée or squeeze the fruit. To the rockmelon and the passionfruit, add a little champagne. Bring the mixture to the boil and skim any residue. Add sugar to taste. To each 500 ml of strained hot liquid, add approximately 6–7 leaves of gelatine. Mix well. Place the jelly liquids into piping nozzles (used as little cone shaped moulds) and set in the refrigerator. To prevent leakage, place Blutack on the end of the nozzles.

For the tuille
250 ml egg white
350g sugar
vanilla essence
300g flour
200g unsalted butter, melted

In a mixer, make a meringue with the egg white and sugar. Add the vanilla essence. Once the sugar is partly dissolved, gradually add the sifted flour. Once three-quarters combined, slowly add the melted butter. Combine well and rest in the refrigerator for 30 minutes.

Spread the tuille mixture thinly with a palette knife into round templates about 3.5 cm in diameter. Place into a preheated 180°C oven and cook until golden brown. Remove from the tray and cool flat. Store in an airtight container.

For the papaya semifreddo

750g papaya flesh

250 ml sugar syrup (made from 125g sugar dissolved in 125 ml boiling water)

Purée the papaya flesh and add to the cooled sugar syrup. Mix well and churn. Form into flat round disks about the same size as the tuille but at least 1 cm high. Freeze overnight.

For the vanilla mascarpone

250g fresh mascarpone

vanilla essence

sugar

Combine the mascarpone and vanilla essence and add sugar to taste. Mix well until the sugar is dissolved, being careful not to overmix the mascarpone or it will separate. Set aside.

To assemble

2 fresh papayas, peeled and sliced

Place a small amount of the vanilla mascarpone on the bottom of a plate. Place the semifreddo on top, which will ensure the semifreddo does not slide. On top of this, spread an even amount of vanilla mascarpone. Place the papaya slices on the next layer and top with a flat round tuille. Remove the three flavoured jellies from their moulds and randomly place them on top of the tuille.

WARM WINTER FRUITS MACERATED IN PASSIONFRUIT ON POLENTA CROSTINI

Serves 12

For the macerated fruits

zest and juice of 2 oranges

zest and juice of 2 lemons

1.5 litres passionfruit juice

1 bottle dessert wine

125g English Breakfast tea leaves

100g dried figs

100g prunes

100g raisins

100g sultanas

100g dried pear

100g dates

2 vanilla beans

Bring the orange and lemon zest and juice, passionfruit juice, dessert wine and the tea leaves to the boil. Strain through muslin. Add all of the fruit except the dates and the vanilla beans. Reduce the heat and cook until soft. Remove from the heat and add the dates. Cool.

For the polenta crostini

450g unsalted butter

450g caster sugar

450g ground almonds

1 capful vanilla essence

6 eggs

zest and juice of 4 lemons

225g polenta flour

1 $1/2$ teaspoons baking powder

$1/4$ teaspoon salt

mascarpone

Cream the butter and sugar until pale. Fold in the ground almonds and vanilla. Slowly add the eggs one at a time and fold in lemon zest and juice, polenta flour, baking powder and salt. Mix well. Place in a tin and bake in a 180°C oven for 40–45 minutes. Place the cake on a plate. Spread a thin layer of mascarpone over the cake and pile the fruit on top.

"TO DO A GOOD DISH FOR A MONTH, THAT IS EASY. TO DO IT FOR TWENTY YEARS ... THAT IS HARD." JEAN AND PIERRE TROISGROS

4

RHYTHM

LENTISSIMO

Friday, 7.00 am. There's something a little sad, melancholy and hollow about an empty restaurant in the morning. The ghosts of last night's diners echo through the room. The tables are bare, the starched damask cloths and napkins lie stained and crumpled in bulging blue, green and yellow laundry bags. Around 7.30 am, the cleaners bustle in, sweeping, washing, vacuuming, heaving plastic bags of rubbish, clanking past with crates of empty bottles. The cooking day begins slowly, with steam. The first kitchen apprentice on the floor grinds the beans and kick starts the coffee machine for the morning's fuel. Others seep in. Soon, a crumpled clutch of cooks stand around sipping, swapping stories, about other restaurants, demon chefs, fabulous dishes, embarrassing failures, and their own 'one day' kitchens. A little after 8.00 am. Franca Manfredi sets up her pasta making assembly line on a stainless steel table just outside the kitchen. Flour, eggs, pasta machine (an Imperia R220 manual). She pours out a well of flour, adds the eggs, and begins to knead the first batch of the day. The reason Franca sets up her pasta production line outside the kitchen is that there is no room inside the kitchen. This is the narrowest kitchen you have ever seen, barely enough room for two to pass, about one metre from stove top to bench. Cooks line themselves up along its length in rows, starting (facing in) with Antibar and hot entrées, then pasta, vegetables, grill and meat (main course), larder and dessert. There are smaller kitchens in Sydney, but none narrower, and few doing more meals at peak time.

LENTO

9.00 am. Pastry cook Joel has just fried a huge pile of golden lattughe (crostoli). There are now about 11 people in the kitchen, quietly and methodically beginning prep. A gold band snapper is filleted. Whiting fillets are rolled, weighed and skewered. Franca is making corzetti, pinching the little coin-shaped lumps of dough between her thumb and forefinger. An apprentice is chopping prosciutto for the sauce for pollo in umido. Franca sticks her head through the pass and suggests she cut them a little smaller. Franco is cleaning out a giant stock pot to make tomato sauce. The kitchen staff are moving slowly, chopping, beating, slicing, talking. No pressure. Yet. Over in the office, Stefano prints out the sales list from the previous day's orders. Every morning, every dish and every drink sold is printed out for scrutiny and analysis. 'It was a good day for wine yesterday.' He points to a Parker Estate First Growth at $115; a Penfolds 707 '96 at $170; six half bottles of Mount Mary Cabernet Sauvignon total of $660. He notes with approval ten servings of cheese went out.

ANDANTE

9.30 am. Jamie – head of mains today – brings up two Illabo lamb carcasses from the cool room to break down. Two boxes from Panificio Giglio, focaccia bread and the signature Giglio rolls, are plonked down. Franco is on the phone talking to an Italian supplier. 'Riso Principe Carnaroli. Si. Ciao.' The phone rings constantly. Chef De's black nail polished fingers chop parsley at an alarming rate. Next door, pork belly is being chopped. Pastry cook Joel is smoothing chocolate topping over a torte with a long spatula. 'Vanilla sponge soaked in vanilla milk. Not bad.' Waiter Monique, still in jeans and t-shirt, is distributing freshly filled salt cellars. Franca has finished three pails of corzetti. She pours out the flour for a second batch of pasta.

ANDANTE CON MOTO

11.00 am. Almost imperceptibly, the pace has picked up. Down at the Antibar bar attendant Paul slices and squeezes a big box of oranges and limes. Glasses are being polished and held up to the light. Waiter Kerry is polishing the glass front to the Antibar food case with a big bottle of Windex. Olives and breadsticks are hitting the tables. Waiter Therese slices focaccia from Giglio, sourdough from Fuel. Jamie has broken the lamb carcasses down, takes the cuts to the cool room. Franco's tomato sauce now sits bubbling away on the stove. Next to it a big pot of duck broth murmurs. Good smells begin to fill the air, a mixture of the stocks, sauces, olives, coffee. The cooks are absorbed, they've stopped chatting, they're chopping, grinding, stirring. Nino is tossing a Sicilian octopus, mussel and Ligurian olive salad for the Antibar. Lamb shanks arrive from meat wholesaler Clayton Wright. Franco walks out with a big white plastic bucket of baby spinach heads, which he begins de-stalking to assemble the cannelloni of spinach ricotta and eggplants to accompany the grilled yabbies and tomato and basil sauce. Boxes of cheese arrive from Simon Johnson. Jannei fresh curd goat, Paesanella mascarpone, Yarra Valley clotted cream, bocconcini, taleggio.

SOSTENUTO

11.15 am. Down on the floor, restaurant manager Chris is transferring the bookings from the scrawled and scribbled telephone booking sheet in a neat and precise hand to a larger sheet that will be his guide to the day. Many have requested a special table location. 'Bit quiet today,' he says, 'about 36. We'll probably do about ten walk-ins.' Pastry cook Joel is squeezing little lumps of amaretto mix onto a sheet of baking paper. Potatoes arrive from BJ Lizard. There's a problem. Are they the wrong potatoes? Or is there just a misunderstanding with nomenclature? Jamie, in charge of mains today, walks into the cool room, and reappears with a little round white potato. 'That's it', he says. The delivery guy from BJ Lizard looks relieved. Franca is hanging the fresh spinach pappardelle out over the railing along the pass like washing over a line. Back on the floor Chris is now straightening tables — 'eliminating the wobbles' — ensuring that the lightly folded damask napkins (they're back! crisp! spotless!) are just so between the knives and forks, the tines of the forks level to the last millimetre. The glasses are still being put on the table. They're late. 'Glasses normally get done at the end of the night. But we had to send quite a few back this morning. They hadn't been properly washed.' Chris frowns. Someone's gonna cop it. More BJ Lizard deliveries. Boxes of big white knobbly celeriac with their leaves on top. Apprentice Josh unpacks, cuts them down. 11.30 am. Sommelier Franck Crouvezier (aka Frenchie) arrives in a beautiful suit, crisp white shirt and elegant tie. And Julie Manfredi-Hughes, ditto, but no tie. She's just checking. Waiters still in jeans and t-shirts. Still running around cleaning and polishing constantly. It's lunchtime, so there are only three in the bar, two waiters, a food runner and a wine waiter. Stefano's calling. Franca calls me over to show me two small stainless steel pannikins filled with cleaned Moreton Bay bug meat. 'They go on with a nice fresh polenta, chilli and tomato sauce.' A huge bowl of white lilies has appeared at the waiter's station.

OGNI COSA È SANA AL UOMO SANO.

EVERYTHING IS WHOLESOME TO THE HEALTHY.

GIOVANNI CASTELVETRO

ALLEGRO

11.45 am. Rhythm definitely picking up. Dishes are beginning to take shape, make themselves known. Nino walks out the Antibar offerings: a rotolini of pasta; little balls of goat cheese rolled in pine nuts; cubes of raw salmon rolled in poppy seeds; a chicken with onion; a bean salad of cannellini, green and gold French beans; grilled sweet onions with pan-fried shiitake and grilled eggplant potato frittata. Franca is worried by the stalks on the shiitake. Are they tough? 'They're fine,' says Nino, 'tender, I tried them.' There's more fire in the kitchen. Waiters pour out of the changing room now dressed in their black waistcoats, white shirts, black pants – and, mostly, big heavy boots. Julie looks at the Blundstones and work boots and shakes her head. 'It's the floor,' she says. The old wooden floor is uneven, hard on the feet. Big boots are best. The braised white rabbits for the little rabbit pie that goes with the grilled rabbit loin and parsnip purée are ready, being stripped to go in the sauce. Celeriac is being chopped, ready for roasting; it'll be served with the grilled Black Angus sirloin and red wine sauce. Franco has rolled his cannelloni. Barossa chicken is being skinned and boned to go 'in umido' to be served with the pappardelle. Flames leap as pork ribs are browned. Jamie crabwalks through with a baking tin full of hot fat, 'hot behind!' Everybody curves out of the way. 12.00 noon. Stefano appears in his starched white chef's jacket and takes me down to taste today's olive oil for the bread. It's the first batch of Joseph's First Run, made by Joe Grilli at Virginia in South Australia. Joe presses the old fashioned way, and the First Run is the oil that seeps out when the olives are piled up on the crusher, often called the fiore. Only 1500 bottles were made this year. It is sensational.

ALLEGRO CON BRIO

12.05 pm. Floor briefing. All the floor staff, plus Stefano, Franck are included. Chris runs the briefing. 'Therese, that half,' he gestures to the front of the restaurant, 'Monique, that half. Amanda, you're wine. Andy's running. Matt, Paul and Kerry at the bar. Kerry can start off on the door. Lots of balcony requests, as no Antibar service out there today. Tables 42 and 40 requested.' Specials are run through. Shortages. 'Only six rabbits.' The wine list has changed, Amanda asks that they study it. Chris finishes off. 'Basically business today, so let's get the menus down pretty quick. Last night the glasses were atrocious – we sent two trays back. That's all. Let's have a good service.' They fan out. Back at the kitchen the chefs have changed into their white coats. Jamie says, 'try this', gives me a piece of rabbit, a little platter of sauce, 'isn't it great?' It is. Full flavoured, a time-rich sauce. I'm reminded of what a publisher once said to me, the reason she loves *bel mondo* is it's not like restaurant food. Joel pushes an amaretto at me, one at Steve. 'Are they ready, Chef? They're a bit soft in the middle.' I like them like that. More importantly, so does Steve. Out they come.

DISCRETO

12.20 pm. First customers of the day file through led by Chris. Five women, expectant smiles on their faces, a glance up at the bustling kitchen gods where rabbit is being pulled apart and slipped into the big pot of sauce. Jamie is slicing the crackling off the roast suckling pig (served with green beans in roast garlic and dried black olives). He hands me a piece. 'Lots of olive oil and salt,' he answers my unasked question about the perfect crackling. On the floor waiters stand attentively, hands behind their backs. Down at table 43, I can see Monique's arms wave as she plays out the menu for the first guests. More straggle in. Herbs arrive from BJ Lizard.

VIVACE CON GUSTO

12.36 pm. The first order is in. Here's how it works. The waiter takes the handwritten order to a computer at the station, enters it. It gets electronically relayed to a terminal outside the kitchen. Three copies, one for entrées, one for mains and one for the caller. The caller hands them through to the kitchen. A capital 'B' goes on the caller's copy, signalling take bread. When entrées are ready, an 'A' goes on the mains docket signalling away, or start preparing the mains. A maximum of 25 minutes to get the main out from then. This first order has no entrées: one beef well done; one whiting fillet; one John Dory; two lambs, well done. Jamie asks Stefano can he slice the 5 cm thick piece of beef down the middle to cook more quickly for well done. Sure. I note that the beef for 'well done' is exactly the same beef as used for 'rare'. 12.40 pm. Sixteen diners now seated. The kitchen is hopping, but almost eerily calm. It must happen, but in all the years I have been observing Manfredi kitchens, I've never seen a temper lost, a voice raised or anyone bawled out. This observation is confirmed by a senior chef at the Australian Contemporary Cuisine course, who visited a number of kitchens to observe them at first hand. He was amazed at how Manfredi staff managed to work in their 'on stage' environment and stay so reasonable. Perhaps there is a connection. Chris tells Stefano a regular has rung and booked. Stefano calls Jamie over. 'He likes rack of lamb – do you have any?' It isn't on the menu. 'Yes, Chef. In the cool room.' 'OK. Don't do anything yet, what he'll do is, order lamb, expecting a rack, he doesn't get it, he'll complain – but he won't tell you he wants the rack.' Another order rolls out of the machine: king prawns; beef; cannelloni; linguine. The well done beef is ready, plated with the roast celeriac. The fillets of John Dory with the borlotti beans and artichokes. Plates are carefully wiped around the rims. A rotolo of whiting comes out of the oven. The skewer is removed. It's arranged with four thick spears of asparagus. The first order goes out at 12.53 pm. They're off. I leave at 12.55 pm. There are now 80 diners. Around 40 walk-ins. Chris shrugs. 'It happens.'

'At the end of the meal appeared a rum jelly. This was the Prince's favourite pudding, and the Princess had been careful to order it early that morning for favours granted. It was rather threatening at first sight, shaped like a tower with bastions and battlements and smooth slippery walls impossible to scale, garrisoned by red and green cherries and pistachio nuts; but into its transparent and quivering flanks a spoon plunged with astonishing ease. By the time the amber-coloured fortress reached Francesco-Paolo, the sixteen-year-old son who was served last, it consisted only of shattered walls and hunks of wobbly rubble. Exhilarated by the odour of rum and the delicate flavour of the multi-coloured garrison, the Prince enjoyed watching the rapid demolishing of the fortress beneath the assault of his family's appetite.'

GIOVANNI TOMASI DI LAMPEDUSA

The rhythm of service changes not just with the time of day – and the day itself – but with the seasons. Lunch moves to a different beat than dinner. People are rushed at lunch. But then on Friday, you get a mixture of those who have to get back to the office, and those who want to play all day. If they all arrive at the same time, if they don't come when they say they're going to come, it's a problem. No amount of staff in the kitchen will prepare you for that. All we can do is work hard and explain the problems. If someone is in a hurry, it's a good idea to let the waiter know up front.

It amuses us that the same people who would never be late for their appointment with the doctor, the dentist or the tax consultant will feel no qualms about turning up late for an appointment with their chef.

Seasonally, we tend to eat earlier – and leave earlier – in winter than in summer. In winter we begin dinner service at 6 pm instead of the usual 6.30 pm, neither of which would be comprehensible in Italy,

especially the north, where the rhythm of life has dinner starting at 10 pm, 11 pm – even midnight. It's nothing to sit outdoors at a restaurant in Trastevere in Rome and watch families arrive for their midnight booking.

This is another problem affecting the rhythm of service: different nationalities eat at different times. Australians tend to eat around 8 pm, the English a little earlier. The more we attract an international clientele, the more these problems occur.

'Sometimes I get sick of making pasta every day. And I get sick of everybody telling me how good my gnocchi are, because it's not only that. I do lots of other stuff. But every day, I make pasta.

'So I start with plain flour and fresh eggs, a touch of salt if you want to, and that's it. For fresh pasta, I reckon you need flour with not too much gluten, like you use for pizza or bread. I've tried other flour, but I prefer this one, White Rose.

'I make a well of flour. I use the fork to beat the eggs, and then when I pour the eggs in the well, I get rid of the fork and use my hands, because your hands can feel the texture. If it's too soft, I can add more flour, too dry, I add an egg or two. Sometimes you need one egg, sometimes two. People with experience, they don't have to follow a recipe – eggs can be big or small. Usually I'm a pretty good judge. It has to be quite dry, but not too dry.

'Then I use the machine, a manual not an electric one. And I work it until it's nice and smooth. You can work a lot on the dough before it goes into the machine, you can work the dough for 15 minutes, but I'm quite happy to let the machine do the work – because it's quicker.

'I throw a ball into the machine, it comes out as a strip, I double it over and put it back again and keep doing that until it's nice and smooth and as thick as I want for what I'm making. Then because of the amount I make, I put down some tablecloths and hang the strips over the railing before I put them back into the machine to cut into narrower strips. You can't leave it too long, because if you do it will dry out and the pasta will break.

'The important thing is to cook it properly. Even if the pasta is not perfect, if you cook it properly, you can get away with it. I use plenty of hard-boiling water, but I never put oil in the water, it doesn't mean anything to the pasta – when it's cooked you can add the oil. I don't use salt either, it's the same thing. You can put it on after, or the sauce is salty enough.

'Although the fresh pasta cooks quicker than the dried, you have to judge. Some pasta is thicker than others – also the larger the pasta sheets are, the thinner they are and the quicker they cook – pappardelle need less time than the taglioline. It's deceiving because you see this large sheet and you think it needs more than the little ribbons. Lasagne is different, it's thicker, and cannelloni. And you have to make sure it's not overcooked because it's still cooking when it comes out of the water, when the hot sauce goes over it and by the time it gets to come to the table. But undercooked doesn't mean raw like they do in Italy now, it's so al dente you can't eat it. You have to judge for yourself. This one I'm making now, if I cooked it now, it's in and out in a minute, if I leave it for two hours, it'll need a little more time. Tomorrow when it dries, it'll need two or three minutes.

'Now when I make the corzetti, the ones like little coins, because it's a thick pasta, I use a little oil in the mixture and a little bit of water – a quarter of water, three-quarters of eggs. You can even make pasta without eggs, with water. If I get vegans I can do that. Once you know the basic idea of pasta you can do anything you like.'

FRANCA MANFREDI

SATURDAY NIGHT

It's One of those Saturday Nights.

We're all waiting for the tidal wave to hit. Waiters are talking about their various outfits for the Sleaze Ball as kitchen staff are sitting on buckets, crates and pieces of equipment, taking some moments of peace and quiet before the first diners arrive.

Everything is ready. All lists have been checked and checked again to make sure all the countless bits and pieces that are needed for all possible permutations of the menu are ready.

There is a tension that pervades the restaurant. It is evident more in the cooks who resemble athletes coiled and ready for the gun. The tension creates a nervous and disjointed chatter that is meaningless and more to do with the release of energy.

This energy is particularly concentrated as the time approaches a quarter to eight and there is still no food docket taken. We have all been through nights like this and Saturday nights that start late are particularly dangerous.

Anyone who works in a busy restaurant will tell you that Saturday nights are like no other night of the week. In fact, Armando Percuoco refused to open on Saturday evenings when he had Pulcinella, in Sydney's Kings Cross.

Saturday night diners are totally different to those that dine at other times during the week. Saturday night is the traditional Big Night Out for restaurants. Of course I've just made an enormous generalisation and, like all generalisations, there is the inevitable exception but, as a collective group, Saturday night diners have different needs and expectations.

It's now eight o'clock and the first people are coming down the stairs. Saturday night is all about eating at eight o'clock. People on Saturday night are more likely to eat in groups of four and beware the tables of six, as these are the groups most likely to change at the last minute.

The floor staff now assume their stations as the restaurant transforms from expectant, anxious ambience to clockwork-like activity. The beast has been released. There is now a steady stream of people coming through the door.

The experience in the open kitchen is magnified because we are on display. We are seen and we are part of the dining room. Its hum becomes the noise in our ears and we are part of the performance.

Orders come in. There is shouting as tables are called and all at once there is chaos. It is not the ordinary chaos that leaves all concerned hopelessly bewildered, not knowing what to do. This chaos is like an old friend that provides each of us with the cook's drug – adrenalin.

Adrenalin is the restaurant's equivalent to steroids. It makes us go faster, jump higher, react quicker and even prevents us from feeling pain as we put parts of our bodies where no human should – into ovens with seemingly solar temperatures to retrieve perfectly cooked food.

A perfectly cooked squab is returned. The person who ordered it wasn't expecting it cooked 'pink'. It is cooked through. It is finally pronounced 'dead' and after a brief, split second ceremony it is replated and sent out again. You can usually bet that if something is going to go wrong, it will do so on Saturday night.

All tables appear to be going through their first courses at an alarming pace. The dockets now fill the boards above the work areas so that there is no more room. This is the point in the service where it is very easy to lose concentration and, if the kitchen is not working as a team, it will lose focus. It feels like driving a very fast car through a long, dark tunnel not knowing when it will finish, not able to see the light behind or in front.

There is no mercy. In the eyes of the diner, there is no reason why food that is individually cooked from scratch, plate by plate, table by table, should arrive late. One table begins to complain about their main course – the inevitable consequence of such a late start and everybody wanting to eat at eight. Luckily their food is up now.

A plate with some squab bones sucked clean comes into the kitchen with the waiter bearing compliments. Five minutes later a similar plate enters with the waiter saying that the lady thought it 'disgusting'. All work stops to focus on the plate – cleaned of all the squab's accompaniments. The bones had been cleaned of flesh just as the previous plate.

Dessert orders are coming in, overlapping with first and main courses. This is the most chaotic point, where every available space on every surface in the kitchen is taken. Cooks jostle past each other. Pleasantries such as 'excuse me' are exchanged for the familiar shoving and warnings of 'hot behind' as searing hot pans pass close to bare human flesh.

With amazing swiftness the tide recedes as satisfied diners relax. One hundred and ninety people have been fed in a little over two hours. It is one of the fastest Saturday nights we've ever done. A glance around the kitchen reveals a scene like a bomb site. There is food shrapnel every-where. Luckily, tonight, there have been no human casualties. ∎

STEFANO MANFREDI

BEL MONDO MOMENTS
THE GOLFER

Sunday nights are very relaxed at *bel mondo*. People eat early and are usually away early. One particular Sunday night, a well-known golfer came in for dinner with five associates. They were conspicuous as a group because each of the cronies was wearing the golfer's range of shirts, each a different colour. They sat and ordered. Their first courses were eaten and cleared. Our timing is simple. From the moment you sit down to the moment you have a main course, less than an hour should elapse. Fifty minutes had gone by since they'd had their order taken. They had been waiting fifteen minutes since finishing their first course, and the mains were about to go out. That is considered reasonable timing in Australia. All of a sudden, the golfer gets up from his table and begins to argue with the maître d'. I was just plating up their mains and had told the waiter so. My mother left the kitchen and tried to calm the man down. He told her how he'd been all over the world and had never had to wait so long for his food. He also added, on his way out the door, that *bel mondo* would soon be out of business. Meanwhile the rest of his party, looking a little embarrassed, fixed up the bill and followed him sheepishly out the door. I still don't know what was bothering him. My best guess is that it may have been jet lag. His subsequent tour of Australia was one of the least successful of his career.

KITCHEN LIFE

STEFANO MANFREDI

It's a dance,
A dance this kitchen life,
Worthy of Baryshnikov and Murphy,
Lift the lids to allow the light
Wipe the sleep from my eyes
As the black caffeine sun
Causes the shutters to squint
Mocking and inactive, saying,
'Start the dance.' The world awaits
With credit card hunger.
Start the dance, tame the fire,
Wear its scars with pride
Like those of the knife kept razor sharp,
Move the flame, sear the flesh,
Burn the skin till it chars
Blistered and peeling like bloody capsicum.
Keep awake from dawn till midnight,
Caffeine and spliff wait patiently
To fend off time, the only enemy.
While architects construct for history,
Pyramids, Parthenon, Opera House,
We build food's monuments — dishes,
Constructed, destroyed many times over
To nourish flesh and spirit.

CHI LI FA LI ACCOMPAGNA IL MACCHERON CON LA LASAGNA. PEOPLE GO TOGETHER IN MUCH THE SAME WAY AS DISHES.

(FROM THE ITALIAN KITCHEN)

Franco Manfredi is Stefano's brother, and one of the two head chefs at *bel mondo* –

'One of the most important things about the rhythm of the kitchen is that everyone does their specified jobs and doesn't, shall we say, improvise. When you have a fast and furious service, and the running of food and people not playing by the rules, the whole thing breaks down. That's happened really badly a few times, to the point of screaming arguments.

'There is a caller whose job it is to co-ordinate the food. Let's suppose somebody decides to bypass the caller and says, oh, I can see what's happening, I'll take those plates that appear to be ready to a table – it can be like a carefully stacked pile of dishes tumbling down around your ears.

'It's such a fragmented kitchen with so many different sections, only the caller knows how the puzzle fits together. There's the Antibar section, which also handles hot and cold entrées; pasta; main course; vegetables and dessert.

'So it's up to the caller to call away the table to the appropriate section, then it's up to the sections to co-ordinate themselves to get the food up and then when the food finally hits it's up to the caller to make sure that (a) everything's there and everything's correctly positioned, plated and cooked and (b) to get the waiters or food carriers to take it to the right people at the right table and you may have anything up to four or five tables going out at one time – and you may have portions of the table ready and you know they may look to be the dishes that belong to that table but in fact they belong to another table and then you have two people on a table having finished their entrée and the other two still dawdling – it's not rocket science, but it can get extraordinarily complex.'

THE ROLE OF THE CALLER

FROM THE BEL MONDO SERVICE MANUAL

To double check pass set up before service:

- printers
- bread
- cheese etc.
- to check with head of every section for specials/changes etc.
- to organise drinks for kitchen staff before service commences
- to double check each docket for number of covers, number of dishes, clarity of special requests on each docket
- to distribute docket to kitchen section
- to communicate any special requests and changes to the kitchen
- to communicate with maître d' about any problems
- to dispense bread according to the dockets
- to direct and co-ordinate the runners
- to monitor the timing/co-ordination and flow of dishes/courses
- to organise plate re-stocking for the kitchen
- to monitor quality and consistency of all food product

RESTAURANT TERMS

AWAY: A dish is 'called away' when it goes from the kitchen to the dining room.

BARISTA: The person designated to run the coffee machine; the sommelier of coffee.

BUS BOY: A plate-carrying waiter – the first job on the floor.

THE CALLER: The caller stands at the pass and co-ordinates the timing of the courses at each table. For example, when an entrée is finished, he or she orders (calls away) the main course. The caller's other job is to make sure the right dishes go to the right tables, and the right diners.

COMMIS CHEF: One up from an apprentice, the first rung on the ladder. Ditto commis waiter.

COVER: One diner. For example, if a restaurateur says they have 'done 120 covers at lunch', they've served 120 people.

DEGUSTAZIONE/DEGUSTATION: A small taste of many dishes.

DISH PIG: Derogatory term for one of the most important positions in the kitchen: the kitchen hand.

GARDE-MANGER: In a stuffy kitchen, the person in charge of what we today call cold larder.

MAITRE D': Short for maître d'hotel, the person in charge of customer relations during service. The maître d' meets, greets, and smoothes things over.

MISE EN PLACE: Literally 'put in place', the setting up of the room and the kitchen and the food in preparation for a service.

THE PASS: Every kitchen has one, the place where the food 'passes' from the kitchen to the dining room.

SERVICE: The time of serving and preparation of meal in the presence of customers.

SOMMELIER: The person in charge of all aspects of the wine in a restaurant: ordering, cellaring and selling.

SOUS CHEF: Second chef, the one under the head chef.

RECIPES

STEAMED ROMAN BEANS, BORLOTTI BEANS AND SOY BEANS WITH AN ANCHOVY AND ROAST GARLIC DRESSING

Serves 6 as a first course

150g fresh soy beans in their pods
1 cup shelled borlotti beans
150g Roman or runner beans, trimmed and left whole
6–8 tablespoons anchovy and roast garlic dressing (see recipe this page)
salt and pepper

Drop the soy beans in their pods into a pot of boiling water. When the water returns to the boil, wait 5 minutes then drain, allow to cool and take the beans from the pods. Simmer the borlotti beans in boiling water for 25–30 minutes. Steam or blanch the Roman beans for 3–5 minutes. Toss all the beans in a bowl with the dressing, season to taste and serve.

ANCHOVY AND ROAST GARLIC DRESSING

Makes about 500 ml

6 bulbs garlic
150–200g anchovy fillets, drained of oil
$1/4$ cup extra virgin olive oil
salt and pepper

Preheat the oven to 150°C. Place the garlic bulbs on a baking tray and roast in the oven until they are soft and creamy inside, about 20–30 minutes. Allow to cool, then slice the bulbs in half across the cloves, and squeeze the garlic out like toothpaste into the bowl of a food processor. Add the anchovies and the olive oil and blend until smooth. Season to taste.

MUSHROOM RISOTTO

Serves 4 as a first course

2 tablespoons extra virgin olive oil
60g butter
1 onion, thinly sliced
1 clove garlic, minced
350g Arborio rice
2 litres chicken or quail broth, boiling
350g mushrooms, sliced
100g parmesan, grated
salt and pepper

In a saucepan, heat the olive oil and half the butter. Add the onion and garlic and fry gently until the onion is transparent. Add the rice and gently fry for 2–3 minutes, stirring with a wooden spoon. Add a ladle or two of the boiling broth, then the mushrooms. As the simmering rice absorbs the broth, add more spoonfuls of broth. Repeat this procedure until the risotto is cooked; I like mine 'al dente'. Remember that it will keep cooking even after the risotto is taken off the heat. When the risotto is cooked, fold in the parmesan and the rest of the butter. Season to taste and serve hot.

ROAST LEEKS WITH MOZZARELLA AND PARMESAN

Serves 6 as a first course

12 leeks, washed and trimmed
olive oil
24 thin slices fresh bocconcini
2 cups grated parmesan
freshly ground pepper

Slice the leeks in half lengthways and cut them in half if they are too long. Place them in a baking dish with the open or cut side facing up and with a little olive oil on the bottom. Sprinkle the cut side with olive oil, making sure that it penetrates the layers of the leek. Sprinkle the bocconcini and parmesan on top and bake at 190°C until the leeks have softened and the cheese has turned golden. Season with cracked pepper and serve.

STEAMED MUSSELS IN A SAFFRON, TOMATO AND THYME BROTH

Serves 4 as a first course

$1/4$ cup dry white wine
2 leeks, washed and cut into rounds
2 cloves garlic, minced
1 tablespoon fresh thyme
pinch saffron
1 kg ripe tomatoes, peeled and chopped
1 kg mussels, cleaned and debearded
extra virgin olive oil
salt and pepper

Place the wine, leeks, garlic, thyme, saffron, tomatoes and mussels in a large pot with a lid and cook over a high heat until the mussels have opened. This should take 3–5 minutes. Finish by drizzling on some of the olive oil, season to taste and serve immediately.

BLUE SWIMMER CRAB AND EGGPLANT TORTA

Serves 6 as a first course

1 celery heart, cut into small dice
1 roasted red capsicum, skinned and diced
1 roasted yellow capsicum, skinned and diced
flesh of 1 tomato, seeded and diced
$1/2$ medium red onion, diced
2 tablespoons Aeolian capers
4 tablespoons of extra virgin olive oil
1 medium–large eggplant
olive oil, extra
salt and pepper
240g blue swimmer crab meat

Combine the celery, red and yellow capsicum, tomato and onion in a bowl with the capers and olive oil. Season and marinate for about 30 minutes. Meanwhile, cut the eggplant into rounds about 2 cm thick. Brush with olive oil, sprinkle with salt and pepper and roast in a 220°C oven for 10 minutes until it is golden and has softened. Allow to cool, then cut 5 cm sided triangles from the slices; 3 triangles are needed for each person. The eggplant offcuts are delicious as a snack, in a sandwich or as part of an antipasto. Mix the crab with $1/2$ cup of the marinated vegetables.
To serve, place a triangle of eggplant on each plate, spoon some of the crab and vegetable mixture on each slice, then another triangle and finally some more of the crab mixture.
To finish, spoon some of the marinated vegetables around the 'torta'.

BLUE SWIMMER CRAB AND EGGPLANT TORTA

MARGARET RIVER MARRON MEDITERRANEAN STYLE

Serves 6 as a main course

1 medium eggplant, cut into thin slices
salt and pepper
olive oil
1 cup tomato and olive oil sauce
(see recipe this page)
2 red capsicums, roasted, peeled and cut into
1 cm wide strips
6 tablespoons roast garlic and anchovy paste
(see recipe this page)
6 tablespoons pesto (see recipe page 33)
6 marron, each about 300–350g, cooked, shelled
and halved
6 teaspoons Aeolian capers, rinsed

Place the eggplant slices on a tea towel and
sprinkle some salt on both sides. Leave for 10
minutes, then pat dry. In a pan, heat some olive
oil and fry the eggplant until golden brown.
Set aside. On serving plates, spoon on the tomato
sauce, place 4–5 eggplant slices and 4–5 slices
of roast capsicum on, spoon on the roast garlic
and anchovy paste in little piles and scatter the
pesto over. In a frypan heat some olive oil and
sear each of the marron pieces on both sides
quickly until they are heated. Season to taste and
put one on each of the prepared plates. Sprinkle
on the capers and serve immediately.

TOMATO AND OLIVE OIL SAUCE

Ingredients

2 kg ripe tomatoes, peeled and mashed in
a blender
$1/2$ cup extra virgin olive oil
salt and pepper

Sieve the mashed tomatoes then place them in a
pot. Heat the purée until it is almost boiling.
Remove from the heat and whisk in the olive oil a
little at a time until it is well incorporated.
Season to taste and allow to cool before using.

ROAST GARLIC AND ANCHOVY PASTE

Makes 1 cup

4 whole bulbs garlic, unpeeled
6 tablespoons extra virgin olive oil
6 anchovy fillets, finely chopped
salt and pepper

Roast the garlic bulbs on a tray in a preheated
oven at 100°C for 30–45 minutes until they are
soft. Cut the bulbs in half and squeeze the garlic
out like toothpaste into a bowl. Mash with a fork,
add the olive oil and the anchovies, season to
taste and mix thoroughly.

PAN-FRIED WHITING FILLETS WITH OLIVES AND CAPER SALAD

Serves 4 as a main course

4 x 350–400g whiting, filleted
8 tablespoons extra virgin olive oil
$1/2$ cup pitted green and black olives, chopped
1 tablespoon chopped capers
young salad greens
salt and pepper

Pan-fry the whiting fillets on both sides in 2
tablespoons of the olive oil. Add the remaining
olive oil to the chopped olives and the capers.
Serve the fillets with the salad leaves and dress
with the olive oil, caper and olive dressing.
Season to taste and serve.

PAN-FRIED WHITING FILLETS WITH OLIVES AND CAPER SALAD

ROAST SUCKLING PIG WITH GREEN BEANS IN ROAST GARLIC AND DRIED BLACK OLIVES

Serves 6 as a main course

1 suckling pig cutlet per person, trimmed (roast them as a full rack)
salt
1–2 slices of suckling pig rump per person (roast as a whole piece), with crackling
extra virgin olive oil
sage leaves
3 whole bulbs garlic
250g green beans, topped, tailed and blanched
300 ml veal demiglace (see veal stock recipe page 39)
100g Italian dried black olives
salt and pepper

Take the pork skin from the rack, making sure it has the fat attached to it. Salt the skin and place it skin side down on a baking dish. Coat the rack and the rump in a little extra virgin olive oil and place on a baking tray on top of a couple of sprigs of sage. Roast in a preheated 220°C oven. At the same time roast the garlic bulbs until they are soft. Remove the crackling once it has formed, about 15–20 minutes. Roast the rack and the rump for 20–25 minutes until medium rare. Rest for at least 10 minutes covered in kitchen foil. Peel each garlic clove and toss with the blanched beans. Slice the rack and the rump and distribute among the plates with the crackling. Heat the veal demiglace, then add the pitted olives and some more sage leaves. Season to taste and serve with the beans and the roast suckling pig.

ROAST BAROSSA VALLEY CHICKEN PALERMO STYLE

Serves 6–8 as a main course

For the sauce
2 cloves garlic, minced
juice of 4 lemons
1 teaspoon finely chopped oregano
$1/2$ cup extra virgin olive oil
salt and pepper

Mix all the ingredients together and set aside for an hour.

For the chicken
$1/2$ cup roughly chopped parsley
4 cloves garlic, minced
1 cup breadcrumbs, lightly toasted
1 teaspoon finely chopped oregano
salt and pepper
1 chicken, cut into joints, leaving the breast on the bone but trimmed of excess fat

Mix together the parsley, garlic, breadcrumbs, oregano and salt and pepper. Coat the chicken pieces by pressing on as much of the breadcrumb mixture as possible. Roast the chicken skin side down for 10 minutes, then baste with the sauce and roast for 5 minutes more. Rest for 10 minutes. Serve sliced with the salad and some of the sauce spooned over the chicken.

For the radish and mixed leaf salad
8 radishes, washed and quartered
80g mixed salad leaves: radicchio, rocket, dandelion etc.
extra virgin olive oil
red wine vinegar
salt and pepper

Make the salad and dress with extra virgin olive oil, red wine vinegar and season to taste.

PAN-FRIED VEAL LOIN WITH SAGE AND JERUSALEM ARTICHOKE PUREE

Serves 6 as a main course

extra virgin olive oil
6 pieces veal loin about 2–3 cm thick
sage leaves
salt and pepper
1 litre Jerusalem artichoke purée (see recipe below)
500 ml veal stock (see recipe page 39)

Heat some olive oil in a skillet and sear the veal pieces for 2 minutes with some sage leaves on each side. Season with salt and pepper, then rest, covered with kitchen foil, for 15 minutes. Serve with the Jerusalem artichoke purée and the reduced veal stock.

JERUSALEM ARTICHOKE PUREE

2 kg Jerusalem artichokes, peeled
50g butter
4 tablespoons extra virgin olive oil
salt and pepper

Place the Jerusalem artichokes in a pot and cover with cold water. Put the lid on, bring to the boil, then simmer for 15 minutes until the artichokes are tender. Drain off all the water, place the hot artichokes in a food processor with the butter and blend, slowly dribbling in the olive oil until the artichokes are puréed. Season to taste and place in a bowl until needed.

OX-HEART TOMATO, TAMARILLO AND SPICED POLENTA TART

OX-HEART TOMATO, TAMARILLO AND SPICED POLENTA TART

Serves 10

For the sweet paste
500g plain flour
200g icing sugar
250g unsalted butter, cold
2 eggs
1 teaspoon vanilla essence

Blend together the flour, sugar and butter until the butter coats the flour. Add the eggs and vanilla essence until it all comes together into a ball. Roll out and line ten small tart pans. Bake blind in a preheated 130°C oven until a pale golden colour.

For the ox-heart tomato confit
1.5 litres sweet dessert wine
250 ml passionfruit juice
750g demerara sugar
2 vanilla pods
10 tomatoes (top off, with skin)

Bring the wine, juice, sugar and vanilla to the boil. Cool. Seed the tomatoes and cut in half, place in a baking dish and pour some of the cold syrup over the tomatoes. Cover in foil and bake in a preheated 120°C oven for 1 1/2 hours. Remove from the oven and place in the refrigerator, uncovered. When cool remove the skin from the tomatoes and discard. Put the tomatoes into the syrup.

For the poached tamarillos
750 ml dessert wine
750 ml red wine
150g demerara sugar
150g honey
1 orange (zest and juice)
1 lemon (zest and juice)
2–3 vanilla pods, seeds scraped
1 cinnamon quill
1 fresh bay leaf
1/2 teaspoon cardamom
12 tamarillos

Add all ingredients (except the tamarillos) into a saucepan. Bring to the boil and reduce by half. Peel and cut the tamarillos into quarters. Add to reduced liquid and bring back to the boil. Simmer for 4–5 minutes. Remove from the heat and cool.

For the sweet spicy polenta
3 cups milk
1 cinnamon quill
3 cloves
6 cardamom pods
150g honey
1 cup polenta

Place the milk, spices and honey in a large saucepan and bring to the boil. Add the polenta in a fine stream, stirring constantly so that no lumps form. Keep stirring until the polenta starts to come away from the sides of the saucepan. Turn down the heat to a very low simmer, cover the saucepan with a lid and cook for about 25 minutes, stirring well every 5 minutes or so.

To assemble
Fill each tart shell two-thirds full of warm polenta. Arrange petals of ox-heart tomato and tamarillo on top. Drizzle around the tamarillo liquid.

LUCIANA'S TIRAMISU

Serves 12

3 eggs, separated
100g caster sugar
300g mascarpone
30 Savoiardi biscuits (Italian ladyfingers)
3 cups strong espresso coffee
$1/_4$ cup rum
cocoa powder

Beat the egg yolks and sugar together until the mixture becomes pale. Beat the whites until they form fluffy peaks. Mix the yolk and sugar mixture together with the mascarpone, and then fold the whites in gradually. Soak the Savoiardi in the coffee and rum, then arrange a layer on the bottom of a small rectangular cake tin. Spread on a layer of the mascarpone, repeating the process until all the biscuits and mascarpone have been used up. Sprinkle the top with cocoa powder and refrigerate for 4–5 hours before serving.

In early 1984, when The Restaurant was barely a year old, one of our regular diners asked, after seeing tiramisu on the dessert menu, whether it was of Japanese origin. Admittedly, if one had not previously encountered this triumph of Italian desserts and experienced the way its name trickles effortlessly across the palate, it would sound vaguely Japanese.

This wonderful sweet mystery has attained Hall of Fame status alongside risotto, pizza and countless other icons of Italian gastronomy. Tiramisu can in fact be used to gauge a city's maturity in its approach to Italian food. Hong Kong for example has just discovered the pleasure, while most Australian cities have moved on although it does remain a classic favourite.

Its origins are disputed, as are the origins of many Italian dishes. I often think that Italians only disagree about these sorts of things for the sake of a good argument, and as long as there is good food and wine then there is something worth arguing about. What is agreed upon, roughly speaking, is that tiramisu is a rather wet and gooey mixture of Savoiardi biscuits soaked in very strong coffee, mascarpone mixed with a liqueur such as marsala, amaretto or rum, eggs, sugar and bitter cocoa powder sprinkled over the lot. There are variations, some being better than others.

A century ago in Milan the locals had a habit of sipping strong espresso coffee while dipping Savoiardi in a mixture of mascarpone, eggs, sugar and rum. A century before that, to the east in Venice, at that time one of the wealthiest and most important trading ports, ships arrived from the exotic East loaded with all sorts of spices, coffee, cocoa and sugar. It was the Venice of Casanova and his licentious acquaintances, who

needed to constantly renew their energy in order to express their unrelenting passions. The literal meaning of tiramisu is 'pick me up' although a friend of mine affectionately refers to the dessert as 'beam me up Scottie', hinting at the amount of coffee required to make an authentic version.

After an absence of about 70 years, tiramisu made its comeback when, in 1962, Alfredo Beltrame opened the first of his El Toula restaurants in Treviso. The famous dessert was an instant hit and, like all such things, many versions have developed throughout Italy and indeed the world. Ricotta is substituted for mascarpone, sponge cake for Savoiardi, rum or amaretto liqueur for marsala and sometimes even nuts and fruit are included. I can't imagine what the Santa Fe or the Nouveau Rustic movements in America will do with tiramisu.

In the town of Gottolengo, where I was born, Luciana, who cooks at l'Orologio, the local trattoria under the town's large clock as the name implies, makes tiramisu in large trays. As the orders come in she simply spoons a generous amount from the tray to a glass cupola and away it goes.

It is difficult to say what a truly authentic tiramisu should contain. On an assessment of all those I've tried, Luciana's is hard to beat. It always makes me sit up, wide eyed and awake. I've included her original recipe.

MILLEFOGLIE OF HONEY GELATO, PINEAPPLE AND LIME RICOTTA

Makes enough for 20

For the millefoglie
250g clarified butter
150g pure icing sugar
1 packet filo pastry

Melt the butter. Place the icing sugar in a shaker. Separate each layer of filo pastry and brush each layer completely with butter and cover generously with icing sugar. Repeat for 5 layers. Put greaseproof paper under the first and over the last layers. Cover with a heavy baking tray so it does not rise. Cook for 5 minutes at 160°C.

For the honey gelato
200g caster sugar
100g honey
12 egg yolks
1 1/2 litres pouring cream
1 teaspoon vanilla essence

Beat the sugar, honey and egg yolks together until they are very pale. Heat the cream until almost boiling. Whisk in the egg sugar mix and the vanilla essence. Stir continuously over a low heat with a wooden spoon until the mixture thickens and coats the back of the spoon. Cool completely before churning.

For the pineapple confit
1 kg caster sugar
500 ml water
2 whole cinnamon quills
6 star anise flowers
10 pods cardamom, crushed
200 ml warm water
1/2 pineapple, chopped

Boil the sugar, water and spices together until the mixture reaches about 175°C. Remove from the heat once it has coloured and very gently and carefully add the warm extra water. This will splash, so keep your distance. Incorporate the pineapple (reserving any juices) and cool at room temperature.

For the lime ricotta
1 packet ricotta
100g caster sugar
4 limes (juice of 4 and rind of 2)
1/2 teaspoon vanilla essence

Fold the ingredients gently into the ricotta.

To assemble
Break the filo pastry into rough shards and place one shard on a plate. Layer with some ricotta, then add a scoop of honey gelato and sprinkle with pineapple confit. Repeat for 3 layers. Drizzle reserved pineapple juice around the plate.

FROZEN ZABAGLIONE CORNETTO WITH POACHED CHERRIES

Serves 6–8

For the poached cherries

1 kg cherries
2 x 375g packs demerara sugar
1 bottle sauternes wine
juice and zest of 1 lemon
2 vanilla beans, seeds scraped
1 orange, juiced

Bring the sugar, wine, lemon juice and zest, vanilla bean seeds and orange juice to the boil, reduce the heat and simmer for 15 minutes. Pour immediately onto the cherries and cool.

For the zabaglione

8 egg yolks
150g caster sugar
1 vanilla bean, halved and seeds scraped
1 cup sauternes wine
50 ml grappa
300g mascarpone

Whisk the yolks, sugar, vanilla seeds, sauternes and grappa in a bowl over a saucepan of simmering water until thick. A figure eight should remain on top for 30 seconds or more. Cool. Fold in the mascarpone and set in cornetto shaped moulds in the freezer overnight. Place a cornetto in the middle of a serving plate. Spoon over the cherries and spoon cherry juices around.

CARAMEL PASTRY KISSES

Makes 30–35

200g puff pastry
$1/3$ cup caster sugar

Roll the puff pastry into a long rectangle 4–5 cm wide. Sprinkle the sugar onto the pastry and roll it in. Cut 1–1 $1/2$ cm sticks, twisting each three or four times and turning them into the shape of a circle. Place on baking trays and rest in the refrigerator for 30 minutes. Bake at 220°C until the sugar begins to caramelise, then turn the sticks and finish baking them. Cool, then serve with ice-cream, tea or coffee.

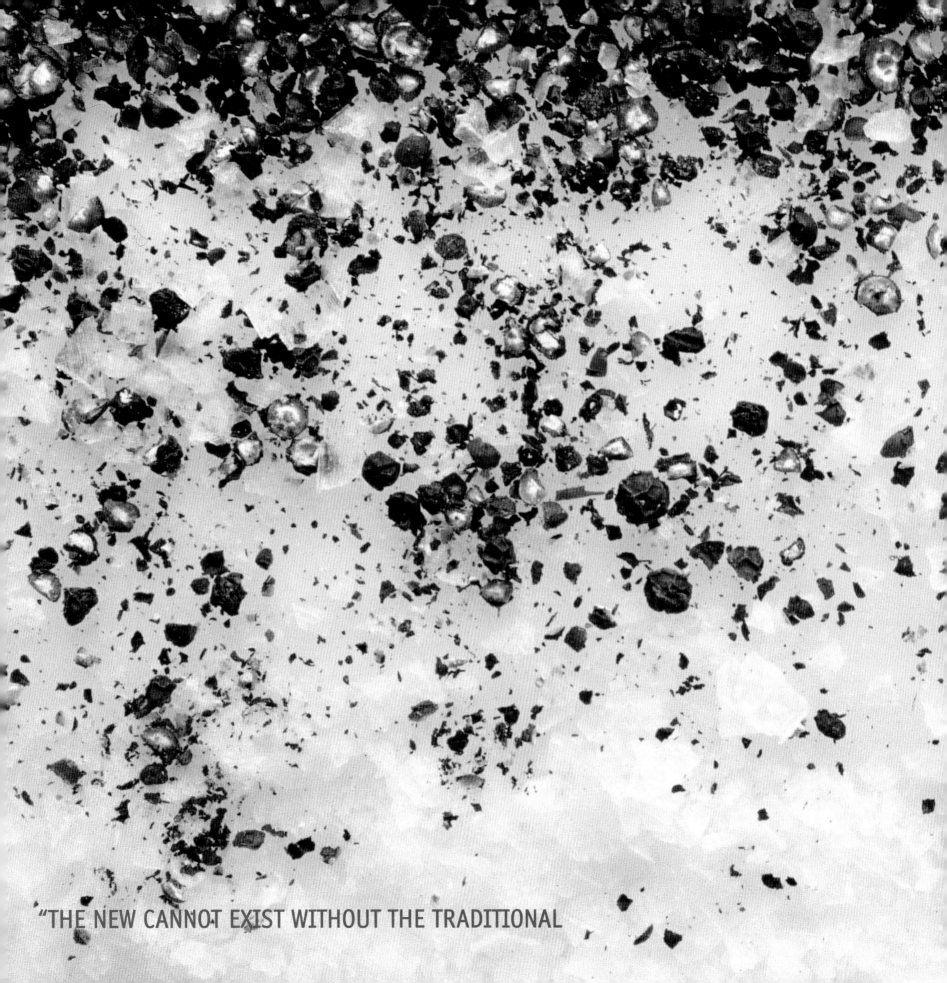

"THE NEW CANNOT EXIST WITHOUT THE TRADITIONAL

5

BALANCE

THE TRADITIONAL IS CONSTANTLY NOURISHED BY THE NEW." STEFANO MANFREDI

A WAITER STRIDES DOWN THE RAMP CARRYING THREE PLATES, SPILLING NOTHING. THAT RELATIVELY SIMPLE BALANCING ACT IS AT ONCE METAPHOR AND DEMONSTRATION OF THE AMOUNT OF BALANCING – AND JUGGLING – IT TAKES TO RUN A SUCCESSFUL RESTAURANT.

It is, perhaps, the single most important quality in the whole mix, beginning with balance in the kitchen. At *bel mondo*, daily, we have to balance between being Italian and being in Australia. Being in Australia means we are confronted with ingredients that are seen as not belonging in the traditional Italian larder. Because we use soy beans and bok choy, does it mean we are not Italian? It's not the ingredients that make a cuisine, but the way you use them.

We toss soy beans through pasta as we would broad beans. Bok choy is pan fried in extra virgin olive oil with a little garlic. This is balancing the old against the new. And it happens all over the world, in Italy as well, as Franca found when she ate soy beans in a restaurant there – an Italian restaurant of course.

A letter from a guest raised some fundamental philosophical issues for me, issues that perhaps are relevant to the way we are developing our 'culture of eating' here in Australia. It had to do with olive oil and its place in the ritual of the table. Our guest wrote: 'The pretentious habit of providing olive oil (yours was of an unsatisfactory quality) with bread is unfortunate ... Four of our table, including myself and husband, had just returned from Florence where we dined at l'Enoteca Pinchiorri. They did not serve bread with olive oil there!!

'I ... have been annoyed at the sudden trend in many restaurants to serve bread accompanied by olive oil and pass it off as an Italian custom. As someone of Italian descent raised in Australia, it is something which was never done in my family nor something I witnessed living in Italy for a number of years and travelling and visiting friends all over the country. I can assure you that it is not common practice in Italy. Italians do not put any kind of condiment on their bread at the table – it is always eaten plain.'

It is necessary to look at this from the point of view of Italian custom first – keeping in mind that Italian customs, especially when it comes to food, vary considerably, not only from north to south and region to region, but also from province to province and many times from town to town. It is true to say that Italians take their bread both with and without olive oil. One can travel throughout Italy extensively and not encounter the ritual of bread with olive oil, but on closer examination one will find that plain bread is dunked into the salad dressing, or is mopping up the olive oil base in a dish of artichokes alla Romana.

At the famous Twelve Apostles restaurant in Verona, we were offered a huge selection of olive oil to taste from a trolley – something I would love to do at *bel mondo* if the floor boards were not so uneven. My own family come from a little town near the shores of Lake Garda way up north. There is a small quantity of olive oil produced there of excellent quality. We always had olive oil on the table to dunk our fennel and our bread into.

On the other hand, travel west to Milan and beyond and you find the French and English custom of butter served with bread. One thing I have learned about my native Italy is that for every Italian who does things one way, there is always one who will do the exact opposite. It is one of that country's most admired and, at the same time, most despised characteristics.

What about Australia? What does olive oil have to do with our situation? If there is anyone to blame for offering olive oil with bread it is the Manfredis. In 1985 we started serving olive oil on our tables at The Restaurant, as it was called then. We had not been offering butter as a matter of course because it had not been part of our family custom to do so at our own table though, if someone wanted butter, they got butter, as is the case today at *bel mondo*. At around that time some excellent olive oil had begun to reach Australia through various importers, mostly from Italy but also from Spain. It was a response to these olive oils and our enthusiasm to give our clientele a chance to taste them that led to the dish with the oil with the bread.

It has taken off like the idea of an Australian republic, though why people would want to claim it is or isn't an Italian custom is beside the point. It has become an endearing custom with many Australians though, like the republic, it annoys some others. It has done a lot to attune people's palates to the nuances of olive oil and has helped to encourage Australia's fledgling olive oil industry. Olive oil is as appropriate as butter as an accompaniment to bread on our tables.

My advice to those annoyed by this practice is to exercise their freedom of choice and ask for the olive oil to be replaced by butter, or to be taken away and replaced by nothing at all – a quite acceptable alternative if the bread is good. As for that restaurant in Florence, l'Enoteca Pinchiorri, of course they don't serve olive oil with their bread — the proprietor, Annie Feolde, is French.

STEFANO MANFREDI

WITHIN EACH DISH, FLAVOURS MUST BE BALANCED PERFECTLY, AS THE TOO ENTHUSIASTIC USE OF CHILLI OR GARLIC CAN RUIN A DISH. AN ITALIAN INGREDIENT MUCH LOVED AND MUCH ABUSED FOR MANY YEARS HAS BEEN BALSAMIC VINEGAR: A DROP IS DIVINE, A SPLASH CAN OVERPOWER.

MENUS

From individual dishes grows a menu, another balancing act. In moving from the old restaurant, we reverted to a more traditional Italian style of menu. From the Sydney bistro style of six entrées and six mains we now offer Antipasto; Zuppa; Primi (first courses); Pasta; Secondi (main courses); Dolci (desserts); Contorni (side orders). Even though it is highly unlikely that Australians would order, as would many Italians, a dish from every grouping, it is, we find, a more flexible ordering of the courses.

Individual dishes on the menu tend to be balanced between one or two offal dishes, seafood and meat, non-meat and non-seafood dishes – you could describe them as vegetarian – usually a couple of birds, sometimes more, then perhaps hare or rabbit seasonally and other things that we have developed with the producers. Illabo suckling lamb is usually on the menu, and now farmed Murray cod and Black Angus beef cuts depending on availability – rump, sirloin or fillet.

The menu never changes all at once; dishes tend to be replaced individually, seasonally, and if something is taken off, it will be replaced with a similar dish, this often for practical reasons because not only does there have to be balance from the customer's point of view, but also from the kitchen's. The workload must be spread evenly in the kitchen, and there has to be a balance of grilled, roast and cold things so there are not too many pots on the stove at once with cooks screaming for pot space.

A menu also tells a story. A story of time, place and the individual. Each menu leaves footprints of the cook's journey.

Stefano says, 'I can look at a menu, and make a few deductive guesses about that chef and his or her origins.

'You may see a menu with a touch of Greek, a touch of Italian and a little bit of Asian thrown in. You'd say, well this person has grown up in Sydney, and has maybe worked here and here.'

Menu writing, in many ways, is as difficult as any prose writing. And, like good prose, a menu description should be clear, concise and simple. It's easy to get carried away and put in every single ingredient, and nothing looks worse on a menu than a 20 ingredient account. The description of a dish should be seductive, but not over embellished. The words should reflect the flavour expectations of the dish, not overstate or misrepresent them. The simple golden rule should be: don't sell it, tell it.

And finally, spelling. We are an Italian restaurant. We have an Italian dictionary in the office to check spelling. If cooking French, a little French dictionary will help, and so on. I've found many of those 'menu speller' guides make fundamental mistakes. I always test them with a simple question: how do you spell osso buco? It means bone (osso) with a hole (buco), and is never spelt 'osso bucco'.

THE MENU GAME

JOHN NEWTON

Discussing this with Stefano, I became intrigued with the points he was making, and threw out a challenge. I'll show you a handful of menus, read out the dishes I said to him, and you name me the chef. He took up the challenge. In my office, I had a folio of menus from 1994 and 1995, ready to go to the New South Wales Library's Ephemera collection.

I read out the dishes, but kept the menu hidden. I began with a menu from a lunch at *Vogue Australia* in 1995. 'This sounds very magaziney,' was his first comment, before pinpointing the magazine – *Vogue Entertaining* – and the cook who'd devised the menu – Joan Campbell. I was impressed.

We eventually did four menus, for three of which he guessed the chef's name. The one he missed, he was incredibly close. It's a new parlour game, a game the whole family can play, and a game that could be played anywhere in the world. I'm sure an intelligent chef in London – a Marco Pierre White, or Chicago – Charlie Trotter – would have the same strike rate as Stefano.

A good menu, like a novel or a film or a song, should hang together. Its parts should form a cohesive whole. Of the Kables menu (the one chef he missed, Serge Dansereau) Stefano said, 'it held together for me because it didn't try to be too clever, it had context, and it didn't ask you to choose the chef, and not the dish. The chef wasn't trying to be a star, but offering food in a generous and timely fashion. I read that menu now, almost five years on, and it still makes sense. That's the problem with a lot of "modern Australian" menus for me, they're ephemeral.'

...IT'S A NEW PARLOUR GAME...

DAY 1

What a day to start this snapshot. Today I've dismissed someone who has been with us for a very long time. The dismissal was a mixture of disappointment on my part and resignation at knowing that this person had let everyone down. I'd gotten no sleep the previous two nights because this was one of my senior kitchen staff, who had joined our team after having finished an apprenticeship. I could only wish this gifted cook well. **Meanwhile I have to clean up the mess. First, I have to notify a cooking school that I will have to postpone a demonstration until November. Second, I have to cover the shifts in the kitchen and third, I have to recruit two people to cover the dismissal and to replace the number 2 in the hot entrée section.**

DAY 2

The advertisement is placed in the *Sydney Morning Herald* for three days — Saturday, Monday and Wednesday. We've found it more effective to run over a week so that we attract the casual readers as well. It reads: **Chef Positions at *bel mondo*: We have two positions available at *bel mondo* for experienced chefs who would like to work in one of Australia's most celebrated restaurants. The successful applicants will be experienced, highly motivated individuals, able to work under pressure in a well-organised team environment. Interested parties please fax résumé to Steve Manfredi at 9241 4763 or email manfredi@manfredienterprises.com.au.** Meanwhile I'm back in the kitchen, cooking for a few services a week and finding the rush of adrenalin stimulating. **A lamb producer from Canowindra dropped off a carcass for me to assess. At about 22 kg dressed weight, it is nearly three times the size of the suckling lamb we use from Vicky and Tony Lehman's property at Illabo in south-western New South Wales. We pan-fried a loin of his lamb as well as a loin of the Illabo and compared the results. This simple test reaffirmed the benchmark quality of the Lehmans' lamb. I gave legs and shoulders away to staff so that they could report their findings and generally we all agreed.**

DAY 3

Meeting with one of our apprentices, who has accepted a job offer in a new restaurant and function centre. I don't want her to go but she has already made up her mind. She has wanted to move out of hot entrées but the position has not been available. I had assured her the next spot was hers but she can see the greener grass. It's a shame because she was highly regarded by all of us as a hard worker and a talented cook. We have a staff of 60 at *bel mondo*. Generally speaking, people are quite happy here. It's a well-organised working environment with good staff rapport. At the moment the kitchen is undergoing a bit of change. One dismissal is followed by a resignation and I need to get rid of some dead wood. **Service tonight was good. I did main courses. We weren't too busy — about 110 covers though they were spread quite evenly throughout the night. It all depends how diners come in. I love the preparation for service. Large, thick wedges of celeriac are roasted golden in extra virgin olive oil to accompany the beef loin. Tiny legs of Illabo lamb are roasted for 25 minutes, then placed above the gas range on a rack to rest for an hour. When they are sliced they are incredibly moist, juicy and medium rare in their pale pinkness. Chris is trimming the large Washington asparagus. They are fat and flavoursome and completely out of season here in Australia. It is one of the few times we allow ourselves to be diverted from seasonality, just because they're so good, the same reason we use truffles imported from France and Italy and also, strictly speaking, out of season here.**

DAY 4

Meeting with Daphne, head of dessert section. There are four people she looks after in her dessert team. Today we are meeting to consider changes to two desserts on the main dining room menu. Figs are on their way out of season, chestnuts are in, citrus is at its peak and the new desserts reflect this. There is a dessert of little citrus tarts with lemonade fruit sorbetto, one of caramel, pineapple and chestnut rotolo and chocolate, ricotta and almond cannoli. Time is set for two days hence. Description notes are to be prepared for the waiters, menu to be changed and printed and dessert section to be shown preparation and presentation. Finally, a tasting is held for the staff so that we all know what we're doing. Very busy night – about 160 in the main dining room and 60 in the Antibar. Smooth night and Franca has prepared a special of 'Bollito Misto'. My description of the dish for the waiters is as follows: 'BOLLITO MISTO: This is a grand dish, traditionally served in winter as part of a large banquet. Bollito means boiled and misto means mixed, so our dish contains a mixture of boiled meats. These are turkey, pork loin, cotechino sausage (made from pork cheeks and belly), veal tongue and Black Angus sirloin, all simmered gently in their own broth along with carrots and baby turnips. These are each sliced and served in the broth. They are accompanied by little dishes of salsa verde, black olive paste and mustard fruits (fruits preserved in sugar and mustard).' The dish was featured in the weekend paper and many people came just to try it – the power of the press. I've prepared a first course special. It is a ragú of wood blewit and chestnut mushrooms with Reggiano and steaming, golden polenta. The wood blewit (*Lepista nuda*) is a wild mushroom found in our pine forests and, though it is mildly poisonous when raw, it is perfectly delicious when cooked. Why would anyone want to eat raw mushrooms anyway? I've never understood the fascination with raw mushrooms in a salad. Their flavour is only coaxed out when they are cooked. The chestnut mushroom is a small to medium parasol, the cape looking like a chestnut, hence its name.

DAY 5

Flew to Wagga Wagga in south-western New South Wales for the Taste of the Riverina where a number of other cooks and chefs and I are demonstrating dishes using local ingredients. I love this region, not just because it is full of Italians, but because it produces such a diverse range of produce. It gives me a chance to catch up with those dedicated farmers who are doing something special, people like Bruce Malcolm, who grows the now endangered Murray cod near the town of Grong Grong. I also caught up with the O'Hare family, who grow the red lentils we use at *bel mondo*, as well as Bill Calabria, who makes delicious wines. I used one of his wines, a 3 Bridges Cabernet Sauvignon, to accompany the dish I demonstrated – roast Murray cod with spinach, pine nuts and sultanas. After the demonstration, Bill told me his stall had been inundated with people who were surprised and delighted with the concept of drinking red wine with fish. My comment on the subject was that we were in Australia and we'd broken just about every other culinary rule and why shouldn't we explore interesting and intuitive experiences. During the demonstration, I accompanied the roast Murray cod with spinach tossed in parmesan. Someone asked whether Australian parmesan was as good as the Italian, to which I answered that it was not and went into details of production techniques, milk quality and ageing. I was then asked the supplementary question of what I thought of Australian cheese in general. My answer praised the handful of world-class cheese makers such as Gay Kervella, Frank Marchand and Richard Thomas but on the whole I put forward the opinion that as an industry it was good at producing bulk cheese for 'cheese on toast' but as far as farmhouse cheeses went there was not a lot of passion, commitment or quality. At the Golden Plate Awards ceremony that evening, held at Wagga Wagga RSL club, the cheesemaker at Charles Sturt University, Barry Lillywhite, expressed the same sentiments. Later in the evening the guest speaker did not. He was of the opinion that Australia made the best cheese in the world and that we should all be using Australian cheese no matter what. I make a mental note that nationalism can tend to cloud judgment.

"OURS IS A PROFESSION OF LOVE AND GIVING. ONE MUST NEVER COUNT THE COST."
ALAIN CHAPEL

But perhaps the most important balancing act of all is balancing the books. Julie, from her vantage point as manager of the whole organisation, can see how all the pieces fit together.

'What's the most important thing about managing the finances for a big restaurant? A lot of nerve. You've got to have a high level of confidence that the money's going to come in. Because sure as hell it's going to go out. But a business doesn't run on confidence: it runs on cash flow.

'I came into this business with a high level of confidence, and we built a debt around that. But we controlled that debt, and we built the cash flow around it. Our expectations were not unrealistic, and we've made a financial success of it. The restaurant is paying its way. It allows us to work on the business, and not just in the business, on the restaurant and not just in the restaurant. We can work on marketing, training and improving procedures. That's important. You can't be constantly chasing your tail.

'But when it comes to things like profit margin on dishes, I work in a different way to someone who was formally trained in hospitality management. I've never learnt the rules. I tend to work in a more organic way. I go for style, and for a certain pitch in the marketplace. It's to do with creating something that is essentially your own.

'Steve is not a scientific executive chef, he runs the menus from his heart. How we decide on the cost is to play with the value/price/volume equation. For example I'll give up volume at lunch – I'd rather have 50 customers who spend $100 a head than a hundred who spend $35 a head. Which means I'd rather not compromise on quality at lunch by cutting prices. At dinner, it's the size of the floor that gives us our strength. We can get the spend per head and the volume.

'As far as the cost of a main goes, I'll go away and do sums on occupancy levels, and spend per head and costs and overheads and I'll say to Steve, we've got to hit this spend per head. And that's how we analyse the menus.

'Because we've been dealing with this level of produce for so long, we've got a pretty good idea of what our food costs are going to be. We know what our workforce is going to cost us, and we know what our operating costs are. So we know we've got to achieve "X" dollars to cover all that.

'We used to start with the 30/30/30 per cent rule, made up of labour, food and running costs. Labour includes things like superannuation, tax, worker's compensation, and running costs like rent, gas, water, menu printing, promotion, replacement of dishes and glasses. But it just doesn't work any more, too many variables.

'You have to walk a fine line between building volume and building spend: if you pitch your price too high you lose on volume, too low and the spend drops, you lose out on revenue which you need to run the business day to day.

'But most important in the whole mix is your customer base. To set prices, you have to know your customer base, know what's important to them. Is it service, or is it value? What's important to our customers at *bel mondo* is feeling valued, getting good service and eating food that is something other than they would normally experience.

In a different market that might not be the case. What another customer might want is good value, something quick. We can supply both of these markets in the same house style, but obviously with different ingredients and levels of service.' ∎

JULIE MANFREDI-HUGHES

BEL MONDO MOMENTS

THE HOOKER
& THE PIMP

A good regular who enjoys entertaining at *bel mondo* made arrangements on a particular day to treat one of his girls. He explained that, as she had just had an operation on her jaw, all her food needed to be mashed or cut into tiny pieces. Consequently, the maître d' assisted greatly with the assurance that the suckling lamb would be cut into minuscule pieces and accompanied by puréed vegetables. Both were very happy and ordered Cristal all evening.

»

"...WE WERE BOTH SERVED WITH A TOTALLY TASTELESS DISH OF WHAT APPEARED TO BE THAWED TAIWAN SHRIMP ... SURROUNDED BY A VAGUE RING OF DRIED OUT RICE ... FOR DESSERT THERE WERE JAM ROLLS IN VARIOUS STAGES OF DISINTEGRATION ... TO TOP IT ALL, THE SERVICE WAS TOTALLY ABOMINABLE."

SAM ORR

Service, as we have discovered in the long journey from being cooks to being restaurateurs, is the key to it all. And the front line troops are the floor staff.

'We need to hire floor staff with basic skills – a dance company doesn't take on somebody who can't dance. You take on a good dancer, you take on a good waiter.

'We have a first contact interview form, and one of the things we rate on that is our instinct about the person being interviewed. In addition to the more tangible attributes – communication ability, linguistic style – we look for intelligence, wit, a certain spunk. Because when it gets hot down there, it really gets hot. So you need people who can shift gear – and do it quickly.

'Our training is mostly in attitude, although there is a bit of

choreography involved. The Manfredi house style dictates that we want you to put things down like this, lift things up like this, put the wine glass down like this, present the wine in this manner.

'And even though we hire experienced staff, when they start, before they go anywhere near looking after a customer by taking a food or wine order, they have to start with running. Which can cause problems, because sometimes the inexperienced people see it as beneath themselves to be running food. I say it's the best way to get to understand who we are and what we do. It's a great way to get to know the food, to see it, to smell it.

'As far as attitude training, there is no script. It is simply instilling a basic belief that the customer is right, that you are not there for your benefit, that you must be friendly and courteous and behave at all times within the

bounds of this relationship. You are there to serve. You're not the customer's best mate. We use the buzz words: accessible, friendly, amiable, set out to please, set out to do whatever it takes to give the customer what they want.

'I guess what I'm describing is the essence of the Sydney style of service – tailored for *bel mondo*. Where does Sydney style come from? We inherited a lot from Europe – we went through that very French period where we thought that was where it's at in dining. And this has been overlaid with American culture – I think the east coast of Australia and the west coast of America, culturally, have grown up together: music, fashion, surfing culture, food.

'Where we differ is in the "hi, I'm your waiter for today and my name is ..." approach. We don't run that system here. We tend to work as a team. I don't believe the customer needs to know the waiter's name. On the other hand the waiter should know as much as possible about the customer.' ■

JULIE MANFREDI-HUGHES

Knowing your customer base is the key to restaurant marketing, because marketing, like the food you serve, has to reflect your own or the restaurant's approach to the customer. Which is why you have to tread very carefully when you do market a restaurant, because even though, in these crowded times, more attention must be paid to this aspect of the business, it must not appear to be too aggressive. Marketing a restaurant is a lot like running a restaurant, in that the hard work should never show in the finished product. It's a delicate balance between effort and seeming effortlessness.

For example, it should be remembered that marketing and advertising are two different activities. It's a curious truth that a restaurant is one of the few services that cannot afford to advertise too heavily. If it does, the question will always be asked by the customers: why does this restaurant need to advertise? In fact, *bel mondo* does occasionally, most recently with one advertisement a week in the *Australian Financial Review* that announced the jazz in the Antibar, and who is playing. It worked for us because the *Australian Financial Review* is a business paper and we're in a business area, and the jazz plays from 5.30 pm to 7.30 pm on a Friday night.

But the core of our marketing effort is, and always has been, four event (and seasonally) based mailings to our customer base per year. Our spring mailing will announce the spring degustation — last year it was the Leopard dinner (a dinner planned around the food in Guiseppe Tomasi di Lampedusa's novel *The Leopard*) and the Melbourne Cup luncheon.

The mailing will also have something in it for our pinnacle customers, a core group of some 100 of our best customers who receive certain privileges. For example, because we work closely with the Sydney Symphony Orchestra, pinnacle customers are given a personal contact to make bookings for concerts and a discount on ticket sales. The planning for this is done by a small marketing group that meets once a week, and has since the early days of *bel mondo*.

A new marketing tool for us is our website, which is as much for our 30 per cent of international and interstate clients as it is for our local clientele. As well as acting as an information medium, it's another service for the *bel mondo* community.

And finally, there is our continuing relationship with the media. 'I believe very strongly that chefs should write,' says Stefano. 'It's no longer enough to tell your kitchen and floor staff what you're doing; that story needs to go beyond the boundaries of the kitchen and the restaurant into the community. I have been writing for various newspapers and magazines since I began cooking professionally. It's also, by the way, a good way of keeping your name in front of a forgetful public.

'A relationship with the food media is a delicate one. You can't afford to be too close to food critics, but I've always made a point of supplying journalists what they want most. And what they want most are stories.'

With the exception of our few advertisements, there is nothing that we do in marketing terms that is beyond the financial reach of the smallest restaurant. In fact, when we started this programme, we were exactly that: a very small restaurant. A very small restaurant whose owners worked very hard to become a larger one. ∎

One of the most complex balancing acts in a restaurant is performed not by the restaurateur, but by the diner, either alone with a menu and wine list or, if very lucky, with the help of a sommelier with the skill of Franck Crouvezier.

Franck Crouvezier is a partner and sommelier at *bel mondo*. Originally from La Bresse, the border village between France and Germany in the province of Alsace, he came to The Restaurant as a waiter after extensive experience in France and England but had always wanted to be a sommelier. After many years of study and on the job training, today he is in charge of our cellars and, in the years he has been closely involved with Stefano and Franca's food, has developed a remarkable ability to match wine with their food. Regular customers will often tell Franck what they have ordered, and leave the wine matching to him.

'The art of food and wine matching has been compacted here in Australia. What has been happening for 200 years in Europe started here around 15 years ago. And there has been in the same time frame a huge change in the way Australian wines are made. What we were producing then were very big, heavy wines. Now we have changed styles to more sophisticated, food friendly wines.

"THE SEQUENCE OF FOODS AND WINES GIVES ANATOMY AND STRUCTURE TO THE MEAL."

MAX LAKE

'Overall, we have a knowledgeable customer base in *bel mondo*, which makes my job rather demanding. They trust the food, and they trust me to understand the wine and food matches. That is good, for that allows me to lead them to discover something new, some-thing a bit more challenging.

'I like to have a conversation first, to find out the food they have ordered, and to see, if I do not know them, any preferences they might have, to see if they have been exposed to a wide range of wines, in which case you could push it a little more.

'But you must also understand when you have 400 wines, as we have, there is not just one solution. So you must understand the person, you must understand the food that has been chosen, and you must know the wines in the portfolio.

'When I eat I choose the food first, and then the wine. For me, it is a visual thing. I read the wine list, and as I read the names it's a bit like a little computer going, oh, this wine this flavour, yes, that wine that flavour. I will review all the wines on the page, go down all the columns until I go, yes, that's the one.

'Say, for example, I want to match a wine to a dish of gnocchi with burnt butter and truffles. You must remember that, as with a meal, the end of a wine is very important. So you look at the end of the taste, not the first sensation in your mouth, and then work your way back. OK, for this dish, you need a little dryness at the end to cut through the flour and the potato, a little acid for the butter.

'Then you move on and say, there is also the nuttiness in the burnt butter, so you need a similar character in the wine, and maybe a little toast, so certainly a wine that has a little age to it so it gets a little development.

'And then you need some floral characters, a little mushroom and earthy character from the truffle. So you need an aromatic wine.

'And then what would come into my mind would be an aged Hunter Semillon, or some of those 1970s Leo Buring Rieslings, from the time when John Vickery was still making them.

'I would not be tempted by an old burgundy, or an old Australian pinot noir, because it would be fine with the first approach of the palate, but the richness of the wine would overwhelm the gnocchi ... but of course there is always an exception, and perhaps a fairly old Burgundy, one on its last legs, starting to get that dryness, but you would have to get it exactly at the right point, with the dryness at the end rather than the fruit to give the gnocchi a bit of space.

'In addition to the analysis, there is instinct, a passion for what you feel that turns into intuition. Sometimes I say to people, this is the wine, and I know it's the wine, and it's good. I know I will get it right.' ■

FRANCK CROUVEZIER

"CONTRAST AND VARIETY ARE BIOLOGICALLY CERTIFIABLE CULINARY PRINCIPLES."
HAROLD MCGEE

You pay the bill. You wander out into the night or day (two very different experiences – after lunch you emerge squinting from even the brightest restaurant like an animal emerging from its lair). You are moving back into the world, the carefully crafted restaurant experience behind you, hopefully content, replete. What was it all about?

Was it, as Gay Bilson famously said (of Berowra Waters Inn), 'just a bloody restaurant'? Or was it, as Joanne Finkelstein wrote, 'a tapestry of private desires intertwined with social opportunities'? Do you enjoy eating out, as Frank Moorhouse wrote, because 'Restaurant eating also allows for very limited social contact' which he likens to ringing someone only to get, with some relief, their answering machine, so that you can 'discharge your social duties without any contact at all'?

Are we eating out more because, as Chicago chef Charlie Trotter told us, 'we're the first generation ever of cooking illiterates – and the next generation is worse'? Or are you, as Margaret Visser wrote in *The Rituals of Dinner*, a victim of the mobility of modernity.

'Modern cities set out so many alternatives – a choice of "stages" – upon which some day a person might hope to shine, and plenty of escape routes for unwanted constraints.'

And you thought you had merely had a pleasant meal, in stimulating company, in a comfortable restaurant. It is indeed a complex business eating out. Especially if you are Anglo Celtic/Saxon.

Fortunately those of us in the kitchen spring from northern Italian peasant stock, which has included now three generations of professional cooks. Eating well has always been important to us and eating out is, and was, simply a matter of choice. Not much choice in Gottolengo, where we came from, but plenty in Milan, our nearest large city – and dining out, at the level we have been discussing, is very much an activity of the large city.

An activity that has progressed beyond convenience and subsistence to become entertainment. Where once you went to dinner before or after the theatre, today's restaurant can provide food for the mind and the body, both sustenance and suspense, sensual and intellectual fulfilment. We follow chefs and their styles as we follow directors and actors and writers and their styles. What's more, the restaurant is a theatre where the diner is as much participant as observer.

While there is truth in the observations of all of those quoted above, eating well and eating out are, more and more, becoming a part of our daily lives as we overthrow our puritanical restraints, and learn that the senses and the intellect can live happily together, in harmony, without guilt, at the table. Perhaps civilisation occurs at that point where the belly meets the brain.

But enough. Just as it is difficult to leave a restaurant where you have had a wonderful experience, and you look up and notice that you are the very last diners and that the waiters are standing around, attempting to look nonchalant but glancing at their watches just a little too often, and you realise it is way beyond time to leave, we must finish this book, which has been so enjoyable to prepare, as our publisher, a little like a maître d' at midnight, is breathing down our necks for the manuscript.

We must do this again. ∎

RECIPES

CROSTINI WITH ROAST GARLIC AND ANCHOVIES

Serves 8–10 as a nibble on arrival

4 garlic bulbs, left whole
6 tablespoons extra virgin olive oil
6 anchovy fillets, chopped into small pieces
salt and pepper
Crostini: toasts made from your favourite bread, brushed with a little olive oil
handful chopped, flat-leaf parsley

Roast the garlic bulbs on a tray in a preheated oven at 100°C for 30–45 minutes until they are soft. Cut the bulbs in half and squeeze the garlic out like toothpaste into a bowl.
Mash with a fork, add the olive oil and the anchovies, season to taste and mix thoroughly. Spoon a little on each piece of toast, finish with some chopped parsley and serve.

PAN-FRIED CALAMARI AND GARLIC WITH GREEN BEAN SALAD

Serves 6 as a first course

3 medium-sized calamari, cleaned and tentacles retained
200g green beans, trimmed
50 ml extra virgin olive oil
$1/4$ cup roughly chopped flat-leaf parsley
salt and pepper
3 cloves garlic, peeled and minced

Cut the cleaned calamari tubes into 2 cm pieces. In a saucepan of rapidly boiling water, boil the beans for about 2–3 minutes until 'al dente'. Place them in a bowl and dress with some of the olive oil, then add the parsley and season to taste. Heat the remaining olive oil in a large skillet pan until it is very hot. Drop the calamari, with the tentacles, in the pan and stir fry for about fifteen seconds. Add the garlic and keep frying for another 2 minutes, stirring constantly. Season and serve with the beans.

GRILLED CUTTLEFISH AND EGGPLANT SALAD, SALSA PICCANTE

Serves 4 as a first course

extra virgin olive oil
250g cleaned cuttlefish, each head cut into tiles about 6 cm square
salt and pepper
500g ripe, flavoursome tomatoes
juice of $1/2$ a lemon
1 chilli, finely chopped (optional)
1 clove garlic, minced
$1/4$ cup basil leaves, roughly chopped
1 medium-sized eggplant, cut into 2 cm cubes

Heat some olive oil on a flat grill or a heavy skillet and grill the cuttlefish tiles till they sear and attain a golden edge – this should only take about 30 seconds per side depending on the thickness. Season to taste and allow to cool at room temperature. Peel and seed the tomatoes and chop roughly into 1 cm pieces, making sure to keep all juice. Place in a bowl with the lemon juice, chilli, garlic and basil leaves. Season and add about $1/4$ cup extra virgin olive oil and allow to sit for 1 hour. Meanwhile in the grill or the pan, add a little more oil and fry the eggplant cubes until they have softened but not disintegrated. Season and allow to cool.

To serve, put some of the tomato salsa on a plate as a base, place some cuttlefish on top and then scatter the eggplant cubes all round the edge of the lot. This dish is served at room temperature.

RIGATONI WITH LENTILS AND PECORINO

Serves 6 as a first course

2 cups lentils, picked through for stones and washed
1.5 litres chicken stock, light veal stock or water
1 celery stalk, sliced
4 cloves garlic, minced
1 onion, sliced
1 small carrot, diced
salt and pepper
600g rigatoni pasta (durum wheat, Italian made)
4 tablespoons extra virgin olive oil
1 cup flat-leaf parsley, chopped
100g pecorino, grated

Combine the lentils, stock or water, celery, garlic, onion, carrot and some salt in a saucepan and bring to the boil. Reduce the heat and simmer for about 25 minutes until 'al dente'. Remove from the heat and let cool. Cook the pasta to 'al dente' and drain well. Reheat the lentils and add them to the pasta. Season with salt and pepper, drizzle with olive oil and add the chopped parsley. Serve with the grated pecorino.

YABBY, SPINACH AND EGGPLANT CANNELLONI

Serves 6 as a first course

olive oil
3 leeks, cleaned, washed and cut into thin rounds
pasta dough (see recipe this page), rolled out into thin sheets
2 medium-sized eggplants, sliced into 1 cm rounds
salt and pepper
1 bunch spinach, washed, cooked and drained well
36 yabbies, cooked and shelled (claws left whole)
2 cups fresh tomato and chilli sauce (see recipe this page)
1 cup grated mozzarella
$1/3$ cup grated parmesan

Heat some olive oil in a pan and gently fry the leeks until they are soft. Set aside. Cut the sheets of pasta into 12 rectangles 6 cm x 10 cm and cook immediately in plenty of fast boiling, salted water. Place the cooked sheets onto wet tea towels. Brush the eggplant with olive oil, season with salt and roast at 220°C until the slices are soft and browned. Spoon some of the leeks on each sheet of pasta, then top with some eggplant and spinach and two yabby tails. Roll the cannelloni like a cigarette. Spoon some of the tomato and chilli sauce on the bottom of a baking dish, arrange the cannelloni in the dish and distribute more sauce over the top. Sprinkle over the mozzarella and parmesan. Season to taste and place in a preheated oven at 170°C for 15 minutes. Serve immediately with remaining yabbies and claws.

For the pasta dough

Make a well in about 100g plain flour. Add enough whole eggs (it should take 1 or 2) so that when they are worked into the flour, the dough is not sticky and not dry. Compensate by adding more flour if too sticky, or more egg if too dry. Cut the pasta dough into smaller workable pieces so it can be easily passed through a pasta machine. Roll it until the pasta is smooth and silky.

TOMATO AND CHILLI SAUCE

2 leeks, cleaned and cut into rounds
2 chillies, seeded and chopped
2 cloves garlic, minced
extra virgin olive oil
2 kg ripe tomatoes, peeled and chopped
basil leaves
salt and pepper

Fry the leeks, chillies and garlic in olive oil until they have softened. Add the tomatoes and simmer for 10–15 minutes. Add the basil and season to taste.

YABBY, SPINACH AND EGGPLANT CANNELLONI

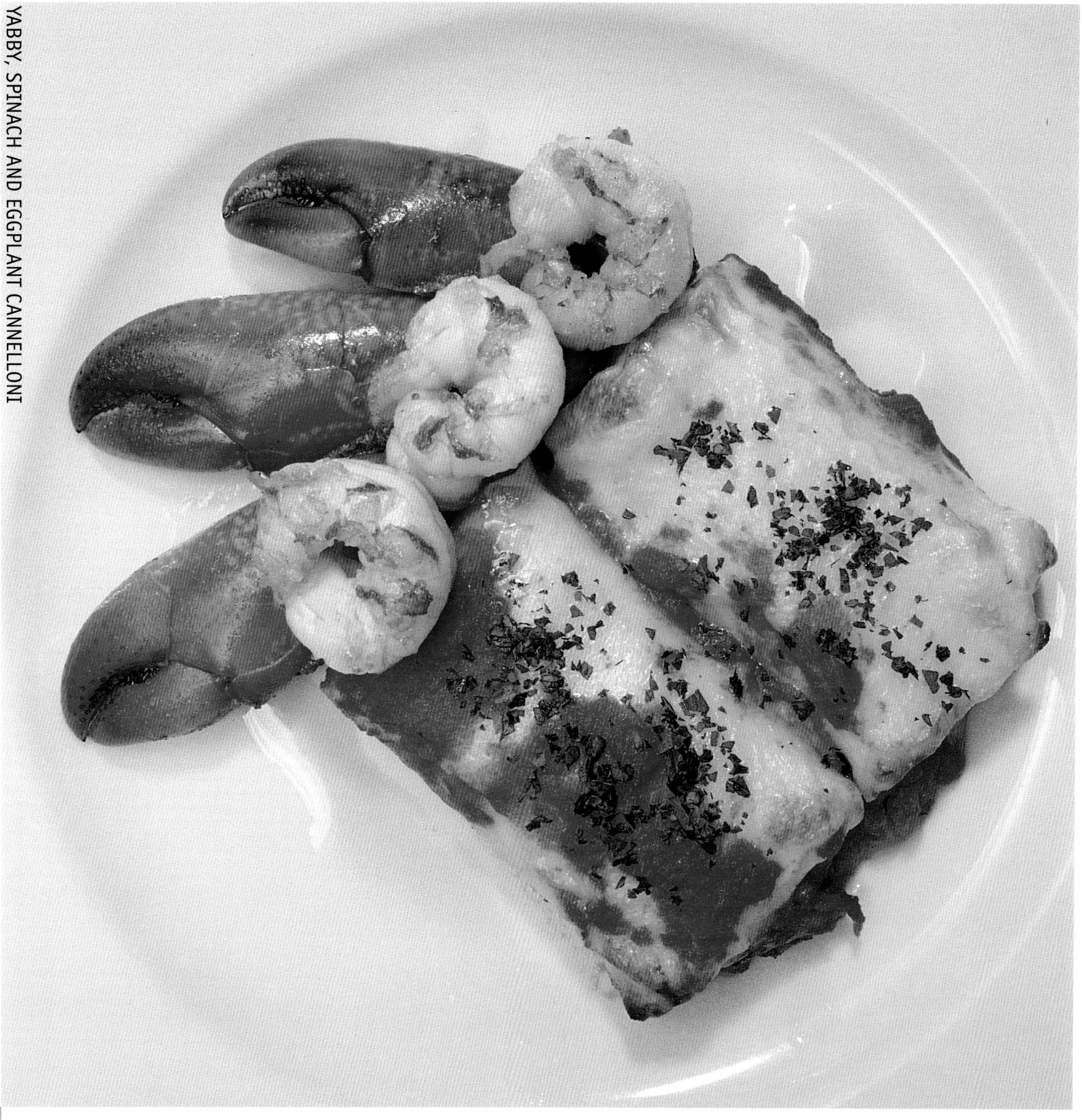

PAPPARDELLE WITH RABBIT AND PROSCIUTTO SAUCE

PAPPARDELLE WITH RABBIT AND PROSCIUTTO SAUCE

Serves 8–10 as a first course

1 onion, cut into 1 cm pieces
1 carrot, cut into 1 cm pieces
1 stick celery
10 whole cloves garlic, peeled
6 tablespoons extra virgin olive oil
120g prosciutto, cut into strips 5 mm wide,
20 mm long and 2 mm thick
1 rabbit, washed well and jointed into pieces:
shoulders, legs, thighs whole and the saddle cut
into 2–3 pieces
1 cup dry white wine
2 ripe tomatoes, peeled, seeded and roughly
chopped
3 cups veal or chicken stock
1 cup roughly chopped Continental parsley
salt and pepper
500g fresh pappardelle
parmesan, freshly grated

In a casserole dish, fry the vegetables and garlic
lightly in the olive oil for 2–3 minutes. Add the
prosciutto and rabbit pieces and brown lightly for
5 minutes, keeping everything stirred and moving
so that it doesn't burn. Add the wine and reduce
the liquid by half; this should only take a minute
or two, as the pot is quite hot. Add the chopped
tomatoes and stock, covering the contents.
Simmer until the rabbit is tender, about 35–45
minutes depending on the size of the rabbit.
Remove from the heat, add the parsley and season
to taste. Allow to cool before taking the meat from
the bone in small pieces and returning these back
to the sauce. Cook the pappardelle in plenty of
boiling salted water until it is 'al dente', drain and
toss with some of the sauce. Serve immediately
with plenty of the parmesan.

STEAMED ASPARAGUS VERONA STYLE

Serves 4 as a first course

500g asparagus, trimmed
4 eggs
2 tablespoons wine vinegar
extra virgin olive oil
salt and pepper
80g parmesan, thinly shaved

Steam the asparagus until 'al dente' and distribute
them on serving plates. Poach the eggs in
simmering water with the vinegar until they are set
but still have soft and runny yolks. Place one egg
on each of the serves of asparagus, dress with the
olive oil, season and add the parmesan.

ROAST BARRAMUNDI WITH DRIED BROAD BEAN PUREE

Serves 8–10 as a main course

250g dried fava (broad) beans
8 whole cloves garlic, peeled
1 medium-sized red onion, coarsely chopped
$1/2$ cup fennel tops, chopped (or 1 teaspoon fennel
seeds)
4 dried tomatoes, mashed in $1/4$ cup water
salt and pepper
$1/4$ cup extra virgin olive oil
180g wild, line caught barramundi per person
50g spinach, blanched, per person

Soak the beans overnight. Peel the skins off, place
the beans in a pot and just cover with fresh water.
Add the garlic, onion, fennel and dried tomato
mixture. Simmer, covered, until everything is soft
and falling apart. Mash with a fork (don't put the
mixture in a blender) but still allowing little 'bits'
for texture. Season with salt and pepper to taste
and allow to rest for 1 hour. It should be of a
soft consistency but not runny. Heat the extra
virgin olive oil in an ovenproof pan and sear the
barramundi for about 15 seconds per side, then
transfer to a pre-heated 220°C oven for 8 minutes.
Remove from the oven and allow to rest in the pan
for 3–4 minutes. Meanwhile spoon some purée
onto the serving plates, then some spinach on top
and finally the barramundi pieces. If fresh broad
beans are available, double peel them and blanch
for 30 seconds and sprinkle a handful around.

DUCK WITH PORCINI MUSHROOMS

Serves 12 as a main course

For the purée
500g celeriac, peeled, cut into quarters
100g butter
salt and pepper
1 whole bulb garlic, roasted whole

Simmer the celeriac in water only until the pieces have softened; do not overcook. Drain and place in a food processor with the butter and seasoning, and purée. Check for seasoning and adjust. Roast the garlic until the cloves have lost their firmness but have not turned to a purée. Peel the cloves, cut each into 3 chunks and mix them through the celeriac purée while it is still warm.

For the sauce
50g dried porcini
180 ml red wine reduction (see recipe page 39)
180 ml veal stock (see recipe page 39)
salt and pepper

Soak the porcini in cold water until they are rehydrated. Heat the reduced red wine sauce and the veal stock in a saucepan. When simmering, add the porcini mushrooms and cook for 10 minutes before serving. Season if necessary.

For the duck
6 x size 24–25 Peking-Aylesbury cross ducks
salt

Remove the legs and the entire rib cage from the duck. Trim the wings off at the first joint. Cut through the breastbone, separating the two breasts bul leaving them on the bone. Salt the skin on the breast and leg pieces well, place them skin side down in a roasting pan and place in a preheated 250°C oven for 10–12 minutes. This will crisp the skin as well as removing most of the fat so that the duck pieces are ready for the grill. Place the breasts and legs, skin side down, under the grill for 5–6 minutes to crisp. Take each breast off the bone, slice into 6 pieces and cut the leg at the joint in two. Spread some of the celeriac purée on each plate, sit the porcini over the purée and place the duck on top of that. Serve immediately.

ROAST VEAL CUTLET WITH ROAST FENNEL AND DRIED OLIVES

Serves 6 as a main course

1 cutlet per person, trimmed (roast them as a full rack)
extra virgin olive oil
3 whole bulbs fennel, trimmed and blanched
200g grated parmesan
salt and pepper
500 ml veal demiglace (see veal stock recipe page 39)
100g Italian dried black olives
sage leaves

Coat the veal racks with extra virgin olive oil and roast in a preheated 220°C oven for about 25 minutes, until they are medium rare, then allow them to rest. Cut the fennel bulbs into 6 wedges top to bottom, making sure not to cut the base and keeping the leaves together. Fill each fennel wedge with parmesan and season to taste. Heat some olive oil in a skillet and brown each fennel wedge on both sides. Finish the wedges in a 180°C oven for 10 minutes. Heat the veal demiglace, then add the pitted olives and the sage leaves. Season and serve with the cutlet and the fennel wedges.

POACHED SPRING SALMON WITH SPRING VEGETABLES AND SALSA DRAGONCELLO

POACHED SPRING SALMON WITH SPRING VEGETABLES AND SALSA DRAGONCELLO

Serves 6 as a main course

6 spring onions, peeled and trimmed
12 asparagus spears
1 cup fresh peas, shelled
6 zucchini flowers with their zucchini attached; blanched and halved
1 side of salmon weighing about 1 kg, skinned and all bones removed
2 litres fish stock
extra virgin olive oil
salt and pepper
1/2 cup salsa dragoncello (see recipe this page)

Blanch the spring onions, asparagus, peas and zucchini flowers. Halve the zucchini flowers and set the vegetables aside.

In a covered saucepan or pan, poach the salmon in the fish stock either as a whole piece or as individual pieces. Simmer until the fish is just cooked through—it should still be a creamy orange colour in the centre. Take the salmon out of the poaching liquid and allow to drain. Toss all the vegetables with the olive oil, season and arrange on the plate. Arrange the salmon on top and finish with the dragoncello as a dressing.

SALSA DRAGONCELLO

Makes 1 cup of salsa

3 slices day old bread, crusts removed
3 tablespoons red wine vinegar
1/2 cup fresh tarragon leaves, taken off the stem
1 clove garlic, minced
1/4 cup extra virgin olive oil
salt and pepper

Moisten the bread with the vinegar until it is completely absorbed. Place the bread, the tarragon and the garlic into a food processor and turn it on, pouring the olive oil in slowly until it is well blended. Season to taste and store in a jar in the refrigerator until needed. It will last quite a long time.

SEARED SALMON PIECES WITH NEW SEASON PINK EYE POTATOES AND GARLIC MAIONESE

Serves 4 as a main course

When new potatoes are in season we like to use them in lots of different dishes. The pink eyes, which are especially tasty and sweet, are a wonderful, dense, yellow-fleshed variety that are also good for gnocchi because they are quite dry.

12 new season pink eye potatoes, skin on, washed
1 cup grated parmesan
extra virgin olive oil
16 pieces salmon, cut across the fillet in fingers 1.5 cm thick
salt and pepper
garlic maionese, slightly runny, not too thick (see recipe page 179)
roughly chopped flat-leaf parsley

Boil the potatoes until 'al dente'. Slice into discs about 5 mm thick. Dust with the parmesan and lightly fry in the olive oil until golden. Pan-fry the salmon pieces, leaving them quite pink in the middle. Season to taste, arrange on plates with the potatoes and dress with the maionese. Sprinkle on the parsley to finish.

GARLIC MAIONESE

Makes about 1 1/4 cups

3 egg yolks
1/2 cup light olive oil combined with
1/2 cup extra virgin olive oil
4–5 cloves garlic, mashed
2 tablespoons lemon juice
salt and pepper
1 tablespoon water

Place the egg yolks in a bowl and whisk until they are smooth. Start to dribble the oil in a little at a time and keep whisking until it has all been incorporated. Now whisk in the mashed garlic, then the lemon juice. Season with salt and pepper. The water would be used at this point to correct the texture to your liking. If you like a firm maionese, then no water is needed. If you prefer a softer texture, then whisk in the water.

STEAMED CHOCOLATE PUDDINGS WITH RHUBARB COMPOTE

Serves 12

For the puddings

250g butter
1 1/2 cups caster sugar
1 teaspoon vanilla essence
4 eggs
2 cups plain flour
50g cocoa powder
2 1/2 teaspoons baking powder
pinch salt
3/4 cup milk
50g dark chocolate buds
finely grated zest of 2 lemons

Cream the butter and sugar together. Add the vanilla essence, the lemon zest, 2 whole eggs and 2 yolks (reserving the 2 whites). Sift the flour, cocoa, baking powder and salt and add to the mixture. Mix in the milk and melted dark chocolate. Whisk the remaining 2 egg whites and fold into the mixture. Butter and sugar some dariole moulds and fill with the mixture. Bake in a bain marie or place the moulds in a baking pan with water coming halfway up the sides and bake at 180°C until cooked.

For the chocolate sauce

200g dark chocolate
250 ml pouring cream
1 tablespoon butter

While the puddings are in the oven, melt the dark chocolate in a double saucepan with the pouring cream and butter. Allow to cool a little.

For the rhubarb compote

1 bunch rhubarb, cut in 3 cm pieces
300g frozen raspberries
200g caster sugar
3 limes, juiced
1 punnet strawberries, hulled and quartered

Bring all the ingredients except the strawberries to the boil. Reduce the heat and simmer until soft. Add the strawberries and combine.

To assemble

Turn out the puddings and pour over the hot chocolate sauce. Serve the rhubarb compote on the side.

RASPBERRY GRANITA WITH BERRY COMPOTE

Serves 10

For the berry compote
350g caster sugar
2 vanilla beans, seeds scraped
500g each frozen raspberries and strawberries

Bring the sugar, vanilla seeds and berries to the boil. Reduce the heat and simmer until the soft ball stage is reached. Set aside to cool.

For the coconut jelly
8g agar-agar
1 tin coconut cream
450 ml water
caster sugar

Soak the agar-agar for 2 hours then drain. Add the agar-agar, coconut cream and water to a saucepan and boil, stirring constantly. Add sugar to taste. Continue stirring, reduce the heat and simmer for 10–15 minutes. Remove from the heat and pour into containers. Set in the refrigerator.

For the granita
1 kg frozen raspberries, defrosted
200 ml sugar syrup
2 limes, juiced

Blend the raspberries and strain. Add the sugar syrup and lime juice. Freeze overnight.

To serve
1 punnet each of fresh strawberries, raspberries, blueberries, boysenberries

Combine the berries with a few tablespoons of the compote and spoon onto a plate. Cut shards of the raspberry granita and place over the compote. Cut the coconut jelly into wedges and scatter around the plate.

BAKED QUINCE AND RASPBERRY PASTICCIO

Serves 6–8

For the quinces
6 quinces, peeled, deseeded and cut into 8 pieces
3 bottles dessert wine
1 bottle water
250g honey
2 x 375g packs demerara sugar
1 capful vanilla essence
2 cinnamon quills
2 star anise
10 cardamom seeds

Combine all of the ingredients in a baking dish and bake slowly at 120–130°C for 5–6 hours.

For the vanilla custard
45g caster sugar
5 egg yolks
250 ml cream
1 vanilla bean, seeds scraped

Whisk the sugar and egg yolks until pale and the mixture forms a ribbon. Heat the cream and vanilla bean seeds until almost boiling. Whisk into the egg mixture and return to a moderate heat, stirring continuously until the custard coats the back of a spoon. Transfer to a bowl and allow to cool.

For the lime ricotta
500g ricotta
3 limes (zest of 1 and juice of 3)
1/2 capful vanilla essence
200g vanilla custard, approximately

Place the ricotta into a bowl and mash with your hands. Add the lime zest, juice, sugar and vanilla essence and mix well. Add just enough vanilla custard to make the mixture wet. Set aside.

For the raspberry compote
500g frozen raspberries
250g caster sugar
1 lemon, juiced
1 vanilla bean, seeds scraped

Defrost the raspberries in a bowl and add half of the caster sugar. Once completely defrosted, heat a pan on the stove until it is hot. Slowly add the raspberries and the remaining sugar with the lemon juice and vanilla bean seeds. Cook for about 5 minutes or until the sugar has dissolved. Remove from the heat and cool.

To assemble
Place some quince pieces on a plate. Spoon some of the lime ricotta mixture onto the quinces. Arrange some of the raspberries on the ricotta. Repeat this procedure again. Spoon some of the compote around the quince tower.

TIME LINE

THE TOFFS ONLY ERA, PLACES YOU ATE IN ONLY IF YOU WERE WELL HEELED, WELL-CONNECTED AND WELL VERSED IN THE RULES. THE DISH OF THE DECADE WAS STEAK DIANE (WITH CHICKEN MARYLAND A STRONG CONTENDER).

THE 1960S: A BIT OF A WASTELAND FOR THE RESTAURANT BUSINESS, PERHAPS DISTINGUISHED ONLY BY THE CONSOLIDATION OF DEMOCRATIC DINING. UNDISPUTED DISH OF THE DECADE WAS THE PRAWN COCKTAIL.

THIS BOOK IS AS MUCH ABOUT RESTAURANTS IN SYDNEY AS IT IS ABOUT ONE RESTAURANT IN SYDNEY. AS WE WRITE, THE DEFINITIVE SOCIAL HISTORY OF SYDNEY'S RESTAURANTS, ALTHOUGH SORELY NEEDED, HAS YET TO APPEAR. FOR NOW, THIS CRYPTIC, IDIOSYNCRATIC 'TIMELINE' OF THE PROGRESSION OF SYDNEY'S FINER EATING HOUSES, RESTAURATEURS, CHEFS AND FOOD FROM THE 1950S TO THE 1990S WILL HAVE TO DO.

ITS PURPOSE IS TO PROVIDE BACKGROUND TO THE NOVICE OR NEWCOMER TO THE SYDNEY SCENE. IT IS NEITHER THOROUGH NOR COMPLETE. WE HAVE CHOSEN TO INCLUDE ONLY THOSE PLACES AND PEOPLE WHOSE EXISTENCE HAVE SOME RESONANCE DOWN TO THE PRESENT DAY. FOR THAT REASON, WE HAVE NOT INCLUDED SUCH IMPORTANT PLACES AS, FOR EXAMPLE, MME LINA HOLDEREGGER'S CHALET, WHICH SERVED SUPERIOR FOOD TO THE GENTRY OF SYDNEY AT CIRCULAR QUAY FROM VALENTINE'S DAY IN 1948 TO 1979. BUT, ONCE CLOSED, IT SIMPLY CEASED TO EXIST, AND SO BY OUR STANDARDS HAS NO PLACE IN THIS LISTING.

YOU CAN USE THIS INFORMATION IN ONE OF TWO WAYS. FIRST, READ IT FOR ENJOYMENT, OR FOR INDIGNATION: 'HOW DARE THEY LEAVE OUT (INSERT YOUR FAVOURITE FORGOTTEN RESTAURANT)'. OR, WHEN YOU COME ACROSS AN UNFAMILIAR NAME IN THE TEXT, REFER BACK TO THE TIMELINE TO FIND OUT HOW THAT PLACE OR PERSON FITS INTO THE LARGER PICTURE.

KINNEIL: Roslyn Avenue, Kings Cross. According to many the 'best' restaurant of the 1950s; it had opened in the 1940s and remained open during the war, where it was designated an 'officers only' restaurant. The epitome of class based dining.

PRUNIERS CHISWICK GARDENS: Ocean Street, Woollahra. Opened in the 1940s and created by Tony Gemenis (whose claim to have invented Steak Diane is a bit dubious), subsequently owned by many including the undisputed king of Sydney restaurants in the 1960s and 1970s, Dimitri Karageorge. Briefly but notably owned and operated in the 1990s by chef Romain Bapst and front of house Remi Bancal (now sommelier at Banc). Then (also briefly) Aldo Zuzza (who worked – again briefly – with Beppi Polese, see below), who came out of retirement (after selling Darcy's) to run it. Re-opened 1999 by Michael Moore, who returned from opening the Bluebird café in London to run Bennelong, which he left for this.

THE CHELSEA: Macleay Street, Kings Cross. Owned by Sidney Newgrosh, it was perhaps Sydney's chicest restaurant at the time. Passersby could look in the window and see the tables set with heavy damask and silver candelabra. Sydney's luxury providore Simon Johnson briefly re-opened it in 1988 with Neil Perry advising. It was Johnson's last restaurant.

CAPRICE: Sunderland Avenue, Rose Bay. Owned by Jim Bendroit, it had swanky showbizzy clientele (Sinatra used it when he came to Sydney). Now Catalina, partly owned and operated by Judy and Michael McMahon since 1994. Chef until 1999 was John Vanderveer, who worked with Neil Perry at the Blue Water Grill (see 1980s).

BEPPI'S: Yurong Street, East Sydney. Opened 1956 and owned by Beppi and Norma Polese, it was arguably Sydney's first serious Italian restaurant (rather than just another spaghetti joint, Beppi served regional specialties) and an important marker in the changeover to more democratic dining. Whereas newspaper proprietor Sir Frank Packer and his cronies dined at Chelsea, his son Kerry and their employees dine at Beppi's. An elegant survivor.

THE BISTRO: Angel Place, City. Opened in 1957 by veteran Sydney restaurateur Johnnie Walker (his first venture was a hotel in East Sydney in 1926). Melbourne-born Tony Bilson's first professional cooking job was here. Walker pioneered a deliberate breaking with the formality of service – away from silver service – a precursor to the Sydney Style.

LE TRIANON: Challis Avenue, Potts Point. Designed by architect Frank Cavalier and decorated by society darling Leslie Walford (lotsa plush) in the early 1950s in what had been home for the Swiss-born chatelaine Miss Rezzonico (and not, as the first *Good Food Guide* has it, Mme Lemesle). Le Trianon was the *ne plus ultra* of stuffy haute style (if not cuisine) in Sydney until 1988, when it was taken over by Peter (chef) and Beverley (front of house) Doyle, then among the leaders of the avant-garde in Sydney cooking. After a disastrous review from Mr Schofield, the Doyles closed down, refurbished and re-opened as Cicada to tumultuous applause. They're still there.

THE SUMMIT: George Street, City. Created by Oliver Shaul atop the Seidler designed Australia Square, the home of the prawn cocktail, and affectionately known as the 'revolting restaurant' (it revolves). It overlooked the growth spurt of the city that began in this decade. Re-opened in 1998 under the supervision of restaurant designer Anders Ousback, with campy décor harking back to its origins.

IMPERIAL PEKING: Not one but a series of superior Chinese restaurants (first at Crows Nest, then Double Bay and the Hilton Hotel and Circular Quay West in The Rocks – still going) owned by (among other partners) Alfred Lai and William Ho. It was important for having introduced Sydney to another style of Chinese food besides Cantonese and for raising Chinese cooking above the simple café level we were used to.

THE FRENCH RESTAURANT: Bourke Street, Taylor Square. Opened in 1959/60 by Dimitri Karageorge, who sold it to his brother Tony in 1962. What Dimitri did was to 'democratise' French food. Now Sydney was offered a choice of pasta or onion soup at this level.

THE HUNGRY HORSE: Windsor and Elizabeth Streets, Paddington. For many years (beginning in the 1950s but hitting its straps in the 1960s) one of Paddo's smartest under the careful eye of Madeleine Thurston. There was also, curiously, and as a precursor to the current spate of cafés in boutiques and nurseries, an art gallery upstairs. Now, and since the early 1980s, the same corner terrace houses a popular Italian eatery, Lucio's, run by Lucio Galletto.

1970s

THE 1970S: PERSISTENTLY FROGGY. THE ARRIVAL OF NOUVELLE CUISINE PUT THE FIRST GLIMMERINGS OF THE IDEA OF MODERN AUSTRALIAN INTO THE MINDS OF THE BETTER CHEFS. DISH OF THE DECADE WAS QUICHE LORRAINE.

THE COACHMEN: Bourke Street, Redfern. In this swish palace of plush, converted from a 19th-century merchant's dwelling, veteran Sydney restaurateur Wolfie Pizem offered middle and lower class Sydney a taste of the 'toffs only' dining style they had been denied ten years earlier.

THE TAI PING: Hay Street, Haymarket. Owned by the Wong family. The archetypal Sydney Cantonese restaurant, favoured by the various cabals of the Australian Labor Party, partly because of its proximity to the Trades Hall in Goulburn Street on the edge of Chinatown, and the racing crowd because of original owner the late Stanley Wong's love of the track. Both famous and notorious, it now trades as the Tai Yuen. In 1972, the Tai Ping name was taken to the Four Seas Hotel, which is currently home to the Chinese Embassy.

THE OZONE: Beachfront, Watsons Bay. A rickety beach shack with the first outside tables John Newton remembers, chef Michel Rey, French, romantic, now incorporated into the gigantic Doyles on the Beach complex.

AU CHABROL: Victoria Street, Darlinghurst. The kitchen here was briefly the home of Dany Chouet (who went on to Cleopatra in the Blue Mountains with her partner Trish Mullene until selling to Damien Pignolet in partnership with Ian Pagent and Greg Duncan of MG Garage in 1999) and her then brother-in-law and chef Michael Manners (upstairs, Glenella in the Blue Mountains and now Selkirks in Orange) and his then wife Monique.

BUTLER'S: Victoria Street, Potts Point. Home to the interesting chef Mogens Bay Esbensen, an early enthusiast for Thai food. In 1991, Beppi Polese's son Marco and wife Norma opened Mezzaluna there.

CLAUDE'S: Oxford Street, Woollahra. Opened by French-born chef Claude Corne and his wife Nicole in 1976, who stayed until the early 1980s. Then one of Sydney's most respected French restaurants. Taken over by chef Damien Pignolet and his wife Josephine in 1981, who continued Corne's high standards before handing over to current owner Tim Pak Poy in 1994. It remains one of Sydney's gastronomic highpoints.

DARCY'S: Hargraves Street, Paddington. Originally owned by Aldo Zuzza, this swish Italian joint was, in many ways, a more elaborate Beppi's, catering for flashy showbizzy types. When Zuzza retired it was taken over by his business partner, Attilio Marinangeli, who still runs it.

FIDDLERS THREE: Military Road, Neutral Bay. Here cooked Cos Psaltis, who later went on to open Balthazar in York Street in the city in the mid-1980s, with wife and partner Toni Richards. Both are currently at the Centennial, a totally renovated pub/restaurant in Oxford Street, Paddington. On the floor at Fiddlers Three was the young Julie Hughes, later Julie Manfredi and now Julie Manfredi-Hughes of *bel mondo*.

LE CAFE: Oxford Street, Paddington. Originally in the Strand Arcade, before fire forced a relocation to the Hyde Park Hotel on the corner of Bathurst and Elizabeth Street. Final resting place, the corner of Oxford Street and Moore Park Road. In all of these locations were chef Patric and wife Chrissie Juillet. Also on this site was Neil Perry's Perry's, then Phillip Searle's Oasis Seros (see 1980s).

PAVILION ON THE PARK: The Domain, Sydney. Executive chef was Mogens Bay Esbensen (see Butler's), then Damien Pignolet, whose star-studded kitchen included at various times Kim Kertesz (Fare Go), Mark Armstrong (Armstrong's) et cetera.

PULCINELLA: Bayswater Road, Kings Cross. Opened in the late 1970s, run by the Percuoco family, father Mario and son Armando in the kitchen. It is often said (especially by the Percuocos) that Mario introduced the antipasto table to Australia. Armando now runs the very successful Buon Ricordo in Boundary Road, Paddington.

YOU & ME: King Street, City. Chef Jenny Ferguson described herself as a 'country cook' and attracted some interesting talent to her kitchen, including Stefano Manfredi and Neil Perry.

TONY'S BON GOUT: Elizabeth Street, City. First Sydney venture for then husband and wife team Tony and Gay Bilson (the landlord the subsequent Tony Bilson associate Leon Fink), described by Leo Schofield in his 1997 *Eating Out in Sydney* as 'undoubtedly the best restaurant' in Sydney. Clientele included the literati (Frank Moorhouse's *Days of Wine and Rage* includes a long lunch piece), pollies and legal eagles.

UPSTAIRS: Palmer Street, East Sydney. First Sydney venture for the pioneer Modern Australian cook Michael Manners (with his then wife Monique front of house), who opened this place in 1970 after returning from a Swiss hotel school and working as a cook in England. The Manners moved on to Glenella in the Blue Mountains, and Michael is now cooking at Selkirks in Orange. Other residents at this venue included Tony Bilson with Fine Bouche and, currently, Genevieve Copland, still flying the tricolour with Bonne Femme.

THE 1980S: THE DECADE THAT SAW THE BIRTH OF THAT ECLECTIC AND MUCH ABUSED STYLE OF COOKING NOW KNOWN AS MODERN AUSTRALIAN – ALTHOUGH IT WASN'T NAMED AS SUCH UNTIL THE 1990S – AND THE BIRTH OF THE TEMPLE OF GASTRONOMY.
DISH(ES) OF THE DECADE: ANY CHAR-GRILLED SEAFOOD, ANY DESSERT WITH COULIS.

BARRENJOEY HOUSE: Barrenjoey Road, Palm Beach. First chef and co-owner (with Judy and Michael McMahon) Neil Perry handed over the kitchen sometime in 1984 to John Vanderveer, who went on to open the kitchen at Catalina (see Caprice in the 1950s) while Perry went to the Bluewater Grill (see below).

BAGATELLE: Riley Street, Darlinghurst. Much fancied French restaurant of the time run by Jean-Luc (chef) and Beatrice (front of house) Lundy.

BAYSWATER BRASSERIE: Bayswater Road, Kings Cross. First outing for New Zealand born duo Tony Papas (chef) and Robert Smallbone, the Bayswater endures to this day as one of Sydney's favourite and defining eating and watering holes. Papas and Smallbone went on to open the Boathouse on Blackwattle Bay in 1998.

BEROWRA WATERS INN: On the river, Berowra Waters. One of the defining and most influential restaurants of the decade in Sydney. First run, briefly, by Tony and Gay Bilson, and then Gay alone with a series of remarkable people in the kitchen and on the floor — it's hard to find anyone in Sydney's restaurant industry who didn't pass through, or benefit from passing through the tranquil Murcutt designed building. Special mention must be given to Janni Kyritsis, whose culinary relationship with Gay over the years was intense.

BILSON'S: International Passenger Terminal, Circular Quay. Tony Bilson's grand plan to introduce haute cuisine to a sensational site on the water's edge funded by developer Leon Fink somehow never came off. It foundered after Bilson's departure, and then soared again with the arrival in 1997 of Robuchon trained rugby playing chef Guillaume Brahimi, whose solid and (at the same time) sensational food keeps what is now called Quay the darling of the platinum card set — and at the forefront of the French Revolution proclaimed by the trendsetters in 1999.

BLUEWATER GRILL: Ramsgate Avenue, Bondi. After moving here in 1987, Neil Perry began chucking rule books out the window to create what the 1988 *Good Food Guide* called '... a more modern kind of food, somewhat Californian in style, involving lots of grilling and a slew of oriental influences'. Sound familiar? The cuisine that dare not (yet) speak its name.

BON CAFARD: Liverpool Street, Darlinghurst. A singular offshoot from the mainstream of the Sydney Style, opened by the excellent chef Martin Teplitsky (son of the Greta Anna of cookbook fame). Next incarnation was Tabac, with George Sinclair in the kitchen, and now it's Ristorante Riva, with Eugenio Riva.

CHEZ OZ: Craigend Street, Darlinghurst. A bright comet flashed across the sky briefly from the south. Melbourne restaurateurs the Staleys demonstrated yet again how different the two cities are. Chez Oz was for a short time (1987 its apogee) the place to be. But Sydney being what it is, Chez Oz was, by the turn of the decade, Chez Was, and no longer is.

CRAIGEND: Hyatt Kingsgate, Kings Cross. Along with Kables in the Regent, proof that good food could be served in a large hotel, almost certainly due to the presence of a young Paul Merrony, currently of Merrony's in Circular Quay.

EDNA'S TABLE: Kent Street, City. Always bold and innovative, brother and sister team Raymond (chef) and Jennice (front of house and collaborator) were, in 1984, innocently creating what was late to be christened ModOz. 'Who could imagine ... deep fried oysters, Chinese cabbage and seaweed in pastry would turn out to be a delicious dim sim?' queried the *Good Food Guide* incredulously. In 1995 they moved to the MLC Centre and based their menu on native Australian produce. In their new home in Clarence Street, the native produce has been thoroughly and thoughtfully incorporated into the Kersh style.

KABLE'S: The Regent of Sydney, George Street, City. Further proof that good cooking can come from big hotel kitchens was provided by Canadian-born Serge Dansereau, who took it upon himself to encourage local producers to do their very best, often buying entire crops to keep them producing. Serge left in 1999 to become partners with Victoria Alexander at the refurbished and enlarged Bathers Pavilion at Balmoral.

KINSELA'S: Bourke Street, Taylor Square. After Bilson's, the team of Tony Bilson (food) and Leon Fink (finance) turned a derelict art deco funeral parlour into a three story entertainment extravaganza with theatre on top, bar in the middle and a very good bistro on the ground floor — fine dining in the converted laying out room. A galaxy of stars passed through the kitchen, Tetsuya Wakuda and Darren Taylor among them. Today, Kinsela's is a pub with pokies.

MARIO'S: Stanley Street, Darlinghurst. Ex rag traders Val Gravelis and David Cowdrill opened this clever trattoria on the site of one of Sydney's earliest Italians (La Veneziana) in late 1979 and it quickly became one of the hippest spots in town. In 1996, David and his new co-owner Katia (Val took off to the Four in Hand pub in Paddo in 1988) took larger premises around the corner in Yurong Street and continue to wow the see and be seen crowd, now as Ristorante Mario. The original Mario's now houses Liago.

THE MIXING POT: St Johns Road, Glebe. Guiseppe and Antonia Zuzza (he's the brother of Darcy's Aldo) opened the doors of this cosy Italian spot in Glebe at the beginning of the decade, and in 1998 handed over to the next generation, their children Peter and Patrizia.

OASIS SEROS: Oxford Street, Paddington. Appearing from nowhere (well, Adelaide), the still astonishing Phillip Searle burst onto the Sydney scene to open the first true temple of gastronomy with partner Barry Ross in 1987 on the site of the old Perry's and Le Café. As late as 1989, the *Good Food Guide* listed the restaurant as French, and described Searle's food as 'highly eclectic', the interior as 'harsh

1990s

THE 1990S: 'MODERN AUSTRALIAN' AS A STYLE WAS FIRST MENTIONED IN THE 1993 EDITION OF THE *GOOD FOOD GUIDE*, WHICH WAS COMPILED FROM 1992 VISITS. THE DECADE ALSO SAW THE BIRTH OF THE 'TOTAL DINING EXPERIENCE', WHICH REPLACED THE DISCOMFORT OF 'THE TEMPLE OF GASTRONOMY'. IT WAS ALSO THE DECADE WHEN CHEFS BECAME ENTREPRENEURS AND DIPPED THEIR TOQUES INTO MULTIPLE OUTLETS AND SUCH ENTERPRISES AS FOOD BUSINESSES AND BAKERIES. DISH(ES) OF THE DECADE: RISOTTO ANY WHICH WAY, CONFITED ANYTHING, BLUE EYE COD WITH THAI STYLE SAUCE. TOWARDS THE END OF THE CENTURY, WE BEGAN TO EAT A LOT OF GREEN PAPAYA SALAD, MUCH OF IT WITH CRAB.

and unrelenting' but reminded us that 'serious gastronomes are ... prepared to suffer inconvenience'. Yeah sure. Oasis closed in 1995 and Searle and Ross moved to Vulcan's at Blackheath in the Blue Mountains, a very casual and friendly place indeed.

PEGRUMS: Gurner Street, Paddington. First major gig for New Zealand-born chef Mark Armstrong, who moved to smaller and simpler premises, Macleay Street Bistro in Kings Cross in 1989, after seven years at Pegrums. He's now to be found at Armstrongs in North Sydney, a friendly spot for the local bizoids who love his beef.

PERRY'S: Oxford Street, Paddington. Neil Perry spent from 1985 to 1987 here before going to Bluewater Grill later in 1987.

PULIGNY'S: Military Road, Neutral Bay. Greg Doyle's first solo outing here, where he spent some eight years before moving to his current home, The Pier at Rose Bay. He continues to cook (with co-chef Steve Hodges and a minimum of fuss) some of Sydney's finest food.

REFLECTIONS: Barrenjoey Road, Palm Beach. Greg's brother Peter made his name here before moving on to LeTrianon/Cicada.

THE RESTAURANT: Hackett Street, Ultimo. The Manfredi family's first outing, opened in 1983, first as a café, then as a surprisingly successful restaurant (which changed its name to the Restaurant Manfredi in 1995) until it closed in 1996 before the move to bel mondo. Another kitchen through which passed some very fine chefs including George Sinclair, Kylie Kwong, Matthew Moran and Sean Moran.

ROGUES: Oxford Street, Darlinghurst. The restaurant in the night club owned by the late, great Peter Simpson attracted some real talent to the stove, including Greg Doyle, David Thompson and Andrew Davies.

ROSTBIF: Military Road, Cremorne. Leigh Stone-Herbert, whose home this was in the 1980s, was described by the first edition of the *Good Food Guide* as 'among the half dozen or so really inspired chefs of Sydney'. The restaurant world's loss is catering's gain — Stone-Herbert now runs a very successful private and corporate catering business.

TAYLOR'S: Albion Street, Surry Hills. In an exquisite building in Surry Hills, Taylor's was the creation of Ann Taylor and Ian McCulloch, who ran the business with a series of more and less talented chefs. Either way it was, until it closed in 1997, one of the more civilised dining rooms in Sydney.

ULTIMO'S: Harris Street, Ultimo. Opening in 1986, the first solo venture for a shy young Japanese chef by the name of Tetsuya Wakuda, in partnership with Sean Dwyer.

AMPERSAND: Cockle Bay, Darling Harbour. This ModFrog offering is the keynote restaurant for the Cockle Bay entertainment development and the latest outing for chef Tony Bilson, this time in partnership with ex-hotelier Ted Wright and adman Rob Olver, who are also partners in the Commissary Kitchen, a very high quality food preparation kitchen in the old casino building. The kitchen opened in 1999 with imports Pascal Barbot (from Arpege in Paris) and Haru Inukai (from Robuchon in Tokyo). After six months or so, Barbot returned to France and Bilson moved back (from the head office of Bilson & Co.) as Chef Patron.

BANC: Martin Place, City. The dream team of Rodney Adler (entrepreneur), Stan Sarris (restaurateur), Liam Tomlin (chef), Jan Tomlin (front of house), Remi Bancal (sommelier) opened Banc (rhymes with bonk) in 1997 to immediate critical and punter acclaim, swiftly following up this success with Wine Banc then Prime, Post and the Food Hall, all in the old GPO, the latter in collaboration with providore Simon Johnson.

BATHERS PAVILION: The Esplanade, Balmoral: Winning a decade long battle with the local council has resulted in a bigger, brighter version of the 'old money down at heel' Victoria Alexander designed beach house we had come to love. Now with a serious chef partner — Serge Dansereau (instead of serious hired chefs like Genevieve Harris) — big things are expected from Bathers.

BEACH ROAD: Beach Road, Palm Beach. Annie Parmentier opened this one, then dived out in 1996 to take over the dining room at Palisade Hotel in the Rocks with co-chef Brian Sudek (which she left in 1999 to open Lunch in Castlecrag). For the rest of the decade run by Richard Purdue (chef) and Paul Dawson.

BEL MONDO: Opened in 1996, home to the Manfredi family (chefs Stefano and Franco, and their mother Franca), ex-wife and partner Julie Manfredi-Hughes, and sommelier Franck Crouvezier. In 1999, the same team under the corporate umbrella of Manfredi Enterprises opened four food outlets in the new Grace Brothers city store, most notably the third floor restaurant, Grace.

BISTRO MARS: Rushcutter Harbourside Hotel, Rushcutters Bay. Neil Perry seems to have had more openings than Hoyts in George Street in 1999, this one is indulging his passion (and the current fashion) for solid French bistro tucker.

BISTRO MONCUR: Queen Street, Woollahra. This elegant — and successful — makeover of an ordinary pub in Woollahra, the first venture for the team of Damien Pignolet (chef/restaurateur) and Dr Ron White (business), encouraged them to do a similar job in Rozelle with Sackville, which didn't work out so well: they sold up in 1999. Next venture, late 1999, the purchase of Cleopatra restaurant and guest house in the Blue Mountains with Ian Pagent and Greg Duncan of MG Garage.

THE BOATHOUSE ON BLACKWATTLE BAY: Ferry Road, Glebe. A second outlet for Tony Papas and Robert Smallbone in a converted rowing club has proved very successful.

CBD: CDB Hotel, York Street, Sydney. Canny Roux Brothers trained Melbourne-born chef Luke Mangan and out front partner Lucy Allon opened here in 1997 for owners John and Merivale Hemmes. Mangan quickly made a name for himself as the city's favourite bizoid and celeb (Kidman/Cruise ate here) chef before moving on to even swankier premises, the lilac tinted Burley Katon Halliday designed Salt (Lachlan Murdoch eats here) in Darlinghurst Road, Darlinghurst.

COSMOS: Bourke Street, East Sydney. In 1994, Modern Greek Australian hit Sydney with the opening of a tiny, self-funded 30 seater just around the corner from William Street. Peter Conistis and his mum Eleni were in the kitchen, and the pair of them – one self-taught, one a home cook – immediately picked up a *Good Food Guide* hat. They're still there, but now it's called Eleni's.

DARLEY STREET THAI: King Street, Newtown. It's curious that the most exquisite and correct Thai food in Sydney (a city bristling with Thai restaurants) is prepared by Aussie boy David Thompson, who began cooking it in Newtown in a pub restaurant in 1991 with partner Peter Bowyer up front. Darley Street Thai moved to sumptuous new premises in Kings Cross in 1992, and the pair opened Sailor's Thai in 1997. At the end of 1999, Thompson accepted a position running a teaching restaurant in Bangkok.

FORTY ONE: Level 41, The Chifley Tower, City. In the sweeping space reserved as a penthouse for the now incarcerated 1980s high flier Alan Bond, chef Dietmar Sawyere and manager wife Wendy built a very fine restaurant indeed, later taking space below for Brasserie Cassis, whose opening chef was Banc's Liam Tomlin.

LA MENSA: Oxford Street, Paddington. A chic cafeteria from the team of Stefano Manfredi and supplier of superior fruit and veg to the restaurant business Barry McDonald.

MARQUE: Crown Street, Surry Hills. Interesting late 1990s entry from prodigal son Mark Best, who opened this highly rated eatery after spending time in the kitchens of Alain Passard in Paris and Raymond Blanc in London. A serious young chef well fancied for future honours.

MG GARAGE: Crown Street, Surry Hills. The unlikely pairing of an MG showroom and a kitchen run by the inspired Janni Kyritsis has proved a winning combination. Kyritsis has bloomed in this environment, surprising even himself with his newfound culinary confidence. Instrumental in this successful liaison are Ian Pagent and Greg Duncan, car dealers (Trivett Classic Cars) and now consummate restaurateurs. The attached Fuel is the very model of a ModOz café.

MORANS: Macleay Street, Potts Point. Frontman Peter Sullivan and chef Matthew Moran moved here in 1995, moving out early 2000 to Aria in the infamous toaster building at East Circular Quay.

PADDINGTON INN BISTRO: Oxford Street, Paddington. Innocent corner pub becomes home to a series of snappy chefs, most notably Paul Merrony, Gary Skelton and Matthew Moran, who was there when it was owned by the team of Stefano Manfredi and Barry McDonald. Currently a deconstructed food room at the cutting edge of casual, with chef Marcus Mano.

PARAGON CAFE: Paragon Hotel, Circular Quay. First outing for ex-Adelaide duo chef Chris Manfield and frontwoman Margie Harris, who then opened in another hotel dining room, the Phoenix, in Woollahra before firing up the curvy, pearly Paramount in Macleay Street, Potts Point in 1994. This is their current domicile, where they continue to set high standards at the eastern end of ModOz.

ROCKPOOL: George Street, The Rocks. Although remembered as an essentially 1980s experience, this quintessentially Sydney restaurant, now the lynchpin of the Neil Perry empire, didn't open until 1989 – with a bang. The 1990 *Good Food Guide* handed it Restaurant of the Year and cooed over its 'neo-Memphis' décor (by D-4 Design). The emphasis on style – and its cost (said to be a then whopping $1.5 million) – set the pace for the rest of the field. More importantly, this is where Perry hit his straps in the kitchen, and any muttering about snooty service and over the top design was forgotten in the raves about the food. In the next ten years Perry not only opened (and closed) many restaurants, he also picked up gigs like Qantas First and Business Class catering. At the end of the century, he was contemplating the next move: television. Through all this, he remains one of Sydney's – and Australia's – most interesting and original cooks.

SEAN'S PANAROMA: Campbell Parade, Bondi Beach. Featuring Sydney's – and perhaps Australia's – first eco-kitchen (designed by Virginia Wong See) and puckish chef Sean Moran, whose Italian/Anglo boarding school cuisine continues to please.

THE TREASURY: Intercontinental Hotel, Macquarie Street, City. Another great hotel dining room of the decade, opened by Gerard Medani then briefly home to the peripatetic Tony Bilson, who presided over the beautiful George Freeman designed room until 1997.

TETSUYA'S: Darling Street, Rozelle. If ever further proof were needed that position is secondary to that which appears on the plate, this is it. A nondescript slate grey corner building in the suburbs is home to Tetusya Wakuda, one of the most innovative and exciting chefs on the planet today. This would be a 'temple to gastronomy' if it weren't so friendly and relaxed.

WOCKPOOL: Victoria Street, Kings Cross. Neil Perry's 'Modern Asian' outlet opened here in 1995, replacing the fizzer Rocket (which lasted barely a year) before moving to the Imax theatre at Darling Harbour. Opening chef Ross Lusted, now at the Harbour Kitchen in the Park Hyatt, was replaced most effectively by Kylie Kwong, who moved on to the bills café group.

INDEX TO RECIPES

INDEX TO RECIPES

BIBLIOGRAPHY

Loose Living, Frank Moorhouse, Picador, 1995.

The Pudding That Took a Thousand Cooks, Michael Symons, Viking, 1998.

The Physiology of Taste, Jean-Anthelme Brillat-Savarin, Penguin, 1994.

Dining Out, Joanne Finkelstein, Polity Press, 1989.

The Man Who Ate Everything, Jeffrey Steingarten, Alfred Knopf, 1998.

The Penguin Book of Food and Drink, edited by Paul Levy, Viking, 1996.

The Great Chefs of France, Anthony Blake, Quentin Crewe, Mitchell Beazley, 1978.

'Bad Boy in the Kitchen', article by Luke Jennings in *The New Yorker*, 27 April 1988.

Brainfood, Jean-Marie Bourre, Little Brown, 1993.

Thus Spake Bellavista, Luciano de Cresczenzo, Picador, 1989.

'Don't Eat Before This', article by Anthony Bourdain in *The New Yorker*, 19 April 1999

'Is There A Crisis in French Cooking?', article by Adam Gopnik in *The New Yorker*, 28 April 1997.

The Leopard, Giuseppe Tomasi di Lampedusa, Harvill, 1996.

The Fruits, Herbs and Vegetables of Italy, Giacomo Castelvetri, Viking, 1989.

An Omelette and a Glass of Wine, Elizabeth David, Dorling Kindersley, 1985.

Ferretabilia, Life and Times of Nation Review, compiled by Richard Walsh, University of Queensland Press, 1993.

Food on the Plate Wine in the Glass, written and published by Max Lake, 1994.

Larousse Gastronomique, Paul Hamlyn, 1992.

'What's That You're Eating', Richard Girling, *The Good Weekend*, 8 May, 1999.

Sydney Morning Herald Good Food Guide, 1984–2000, various editors, Anne O'Donovan.

Eating Out in Sydney 1977, Leo Schofield, Angus & Robertson 1977.